PERSONALITY CHANGES IN AGING

PERSONALITY CHANGES IN AGING

A Longitudinal Study of Community Residents

Joseph H. Britton
Jean O. Britton

Springer Publishing Company Inc., New York

Contents

List of Tables

Preface

Developmental psychologists might be thought of as historians concerned with describing, explaining, and predicting the course of human events or processes. Whether they are studying the early or the late years of life, they are attempting to find meaning in what happens with the passage of time.

In *Personality Change and Aging: A Longitudinal Study of Community Residents*, we report research growing out of broad interests in mental health and in what occurs with the passage of time in later maturity and old age. We wanted to know what happens to ordinary old people as they face the everyday problems of living, and what characterizes both those who decline and those who are able to maintain or improve their personality functioning. We wished to discover what adjustments they find necessary or desirable in order to continue a reasonably satisfying and satisfactory existence as they grew older. We thought it important to learn how members of their community and of the organizations in it view them and their problems, as well as how members of their families see them and help them as they try to manage their affairs at this late phase of life. These wide interests in old people led us to more precise questions, including: What is the nature of those people who manage to survive to grow older?

We were questioning a widely-held but empirically-unsubstantiated belief that patterns of behavior and adjustment persist through the later years in spite of the need to adapt to changing circumstances, on the one hand, or because of apparently shrinking opportunities to exercise abilities to change, on the other. In addition, we aimed to identify some of the social-psychological correlates of survival in old age. These problems required a reasonably stable environment with individuals living in it whose lives we could study over a period of time. Gerontologists and developmentalists have repeatedly called for such longitudinal investigations, recognizing many of the serious problems which beset such research. We encountered many of these commonly recognized problems, such as the attrition of subjects, maintenance of their interest and willingness to participate, and problems of repeated measurements.

Our investigations stemmed from our belief that people respond to and are responded to by life events and environmental circumstances in individual patterns, ones that might be described and explained for the ultimate purposes of learning what conditions and environments can be provided for continued well being in later life.

Our intent is to interest behavioral scientists concerned with theoretical and methodological issues in gerontology and in social and developmental psychology. We believe our work is also relevant for professional workers who deal with older persons, individually or in groups or in community action programs.

Joseph H. Britton
Jean Oppenheimer Britton

University Park, Pennsylvania
April, 1972

Acknowledgements

Interest in the kinds of human problems studied in this investigation arose from our own life experiences of growing up in ambitious families whose members felt they ought to try to make the world a better place in which to live. We are grateful for this heritage given us so unselfishly by our parents, J. J. and Florence Greer Oppenheimer and Edgar C. and Grace Van Huss Britton. Similarly, we are appreciative of the traditions of community-based social science research established by our teachers at the University of Chicago, particularly Professor Robert J. Havighurst, and also the late Professors Ernest W. Burgess, W. Lloyd Warner, and J. Carson McGuire.

We are pleased to acknowledge the professional opportunities and supportive environment which The Pennsylvania State University has provided us to pursue these research interests over the years. Financial assistance came from the University's Agricultural Experiment Station, College of Human Development (and before it, the College of Home Economics), Department of Agricultural Economics and Rural Sociology, and its Central Fund for Research, and, in the later phases of the study from the National Institute of Child Health and Human Development (Grant HD 01757). The interest and support of the late Dean Grace M. Henderson are particularly appreciated. As we launched the project, fellow members of the Committee for Study of Adulthood—Professors Rose Cologne, Mary L. Dodds, William G. Mather, and William M. Smith, Jr. — stimulated us in these long-term efforts; Professor Mather became a collaborator in the early phases of the project. Other colleagues, notably Professor Charles Taylor, director of the University's training program in Adult Development and Aging, have, with our graduate students, challenged our thinking and shared their ideas with us. We have benefited from these discussions and from their friendships.

This longitudinal research project has served as a training ground for many Penn State students, as it has also profited by the assistance of many individuals. It is a pleasure to acknowledge our indebtedness to them. Drs. S. W. Becker, Douglas N. Jackson, and

George T. Wilcox helped to construct some of our original instruments. Professor Havighurst consulted with us on the research design, and Professor William S. Ray, now of the University of Pittsburgh, was helpful throughout the study, from its inception to conclusion, particularly in the matter of statistical analysis.

Individuals who served as interviewers were the following: Ruth Anderson, Mrs. Donna M. Baker, Joseph A. Birt, Robert Hobaugh, Mrs. Ruth Hummel, Mrs. Lucile Hurley, Mark L. Knapp, Mrs. Alice K. Lansing, Matthew Levy, Mrs. Grace E. Meserole, David H. Olson, Mrs. Joy Olson, Mrs. Virginia Rohrer, Violet E. Telford, Mrs. Theola F. Thevaos, Marion Vanfossen, Carol Wrieth, and Mrs. Caryl S. Wright. Persons who assisted with the analysis of data included: Jean A. Borden, Mrs. Catherine E. Cameron, Mary A. Cressler, Mrs. Jean D. Davidson, Mrs. Barbara W. Davis, Mrs. Nancy Fenstermacher, Mrs. Nancy S. Gamble, Mrs. Nancy W. Goyette, Alia T. Halawi, Mrs. Mary C. Harrison, Paul C. Harrison, Jr., Mary Heltsley, Mrs. Mary G. Hubert, Cheryl Kaneoka, Garrett W. Lange, Lorraine Stocker, Janet T. Reid, Mrs. Elizabeth T. Reeser, Ronald L. Russell, Anthony J. Traxler, Mrs. Dorothy H. Welsh, Grady White, Pamela Wheeler, and Roger M. Wier. We are grateful for their efforts.

The final writing of the report was aided by provision of a hospitable setting for a sabbatical leave at the Gerontology Center of the University of Southern California; the interest in the project over the years by the Center's director, Professor James E. Birren, is especially gratifying. Mrs. Dorothy Lewis and Mrs. Esther Gollobin, Managing Editor and Editor, respectively, of Springer Publishing Company, and Mrs. Marion Stocker gave generously of their editorial talents.

While the necessity of having to assign fictitious names to our study community prevents us from giving personal recognition to both the participants in the research and the numerous other community members who assisted us in so many ways, we wish, at least, to express publicly our keen appreciation for their help. While the years of study have enhanced our regard for the community and its residents, we have tried to picture the community and the life of its older adults in an objective fashion. If, in their wisdom, residents feel we have been unjustly critical, we ask their indulgence.

We also wish to thank Joe Creason and the *Courier-Journal* of Louisville, Kentucky for permission to reprint portions of Creason's column of September 19, 1969.

J. H. B.
J. O. B.

Chapter 1

The Research Problem: Stability and Survival of Older Community Residents

CONTINUITY OF PERSONALITY AND ADJUSTMENT

There is widespread belief that as a child grows up and becomes an adult he achieves a stable personality and an adjustment pattern that persists throughout the rest of his life. According to this belief, arrival at adulthood signals fulfillment of the promise of the unfolding process of growth and maturation. Childish and erratic ways are discarded; the adult behaves consistently with his own unique pattern of behavior. In the opinion of some writers, such stability marks the person as mature and healthy (Heath, 1965). Presumably some years of maturity follow during which he continues in his own individual pattern but grows older and begins to age.

This description of development and aging over the life span may be the popular belief, but until demonstrated as fact, it must remain a postulation. The process of change from erratic childhood to consistent maturity has been neither well formulated theoretically nor substantiated with empirical data. Nor has the degree of consistency throughout the adult years and into old age been demonstrated.

While it might be possible to define maturity in reference to stability, it appears that a dynamic pattern of behavior that enables the individual to adapt and to accommodate himself to changing needs and circumstances would certainly be useful. One author has stressed the *perpetual change* of behavior as characterizing the living organism:

> The behavior of animal and man is a continuous stream of activity from fertilization to death. In such a continuous process of energy exchange between the organism and the [ever-changing] environment, behavior never comes to an end. If there is an end in behavior, that end must be death, for death is the end of all ends (Kuo, 1967, p. 13).

Such dynamic change and adaptability, accompanied by an endless variety of behavior patterns, are related to the very processes of *surviving* and hence to the processes of *development* and *aging*. Actually, the concepts of "development" and "aging" (Bortner, 1966, 1967; Taylor, 1971) imply processes of change that occur during the course of living and surviving through time. According to Nagel (1957), development connotes a system with "pre-existing capabilities" which goes through "sequential changes" and yields *"relatively permanent* novel increments not only in structure but in . . . modes of operation" (p. 17; emphasis added). Aging begins, Birren has said, "when the forces of growth bring the organism to a *relative equilibrium"* (Birren, 1964, p. 2; emphasis added).

In his analysis, *Stability and Change in Human Characteristics,* Bloom (1964) suggested that "basic mechanisms and processes" are most likely to be stable, whereas "symptoms and more superficial aspects of an individual's behavior" are less likely to be stable: "unconscious and deep-seated characteristics are difficult to change, whereas highly conscious and more nearly surface aspects of human behavior and personality may be more subject to change and are therefore less stable" (p. 5). Bloom called for empirical studies of developing and changing characteristics *and* of changing environments, and said:

> What forces and processes keep a characteristic from changing and what forces and processes develop the characteristic further, *even after periods when normally it would be considered fully formed?* Are there some periods in the life stages of an individual when a characteristic can become markedly reorganized . . . ? (Bloom, 1964, p. 223; emphasis added).

The Issue of Personality Change

The present research was undertaken to study the degree of equilibrium or consistency of personality and adjustment in a group of older persons over a decade in their later years of life. The inquiry was related to these questions: How permanent are the increments of the developing years? How far does equilibrium extend into old age?

Subjects aged 65 and over were interviewed and tested on three occasions over a nine-year period, and the extent of consistency or change over that period was determined. The dimensions investigated were *personality* and *adjustment*, two aspects of human behavior which carry a wide variety of meanings. Personality and adjustment are typically assessed by a wide variety of methods. Our use of the terms here follows certain conceptual and methodological restraints which are important to keep in mind throughout this report.

Personality may be defined as by Chown: "the gestalt of the individual's attitudes, emotions, motivations, and activity patterns—the impression a man makes on others and the impression he makes on himself" (Chown, 1968, p. 134). This broad definition includes, for example, the ways in which the individual uses his cognitive and motor abilities in his everyday life, within his particular physical, economic, and social environment. Thus, personality may be thought of as the distinctive pattern of organizing one's perceptions and beliefs, as well as ways of acting and reacting (English and English, 1958).

Adjustment is a process by which the individual person (personality) relates to his environment in such ways as to satisfy most of his own needs and to meet the demands placed upon him (English and English, 1958).

The concepts of personality and adjustment are closely related. In fact, personality may be thought of as an adjustment pattern, a set of typical ways in which an individual with certain personality characteristics functions as a whole so as to meet his own needs and the expectations others have for him. (In certain respects, also, adjustment might be thought of as a dependent variable of personality.) In the present report we often use the terms interchangeably, partly because the measures employed are operationally defined in both ways. A measure such as an attitude inventory seems to describe the characteristics of a person in interaction with his environment and, at the same time, to show the extent to which he derives satisfaction from his interactions and meets the demands made upon him by others.

Stability of personality and adjustment involves the extent to which there is persistence or change in these areas over a period of time—in our study, over a period of years in the latter part of life. In view of the need for adaptation in the face of changing circumstances, we emphasize that stability of personality and adjustment is a relative matter. What is stable and persistent is not necessarily brittle and inflexible. In fact, during later maturity and old age, important changes take place in the individual and in the ways society views him. Hence the manner in which he views himself and the ways in which he acts may have to change quite radically. Nevertheless the basic pattern of adjustment, or the gestalt of his personality, persists, with only minor changes or variations occurring within the pervading "theme."

Personality Formation

The possibility that change could occur in personality and adjustment in adulthood relates to the question of how personality is formed: What factors contribute to personality development? What determines the nature of an adjustment pattern? In a classic statement, Kluckhohn and Murray (1948) claimed that personality is formed by constitutional, group membership, role, and situational determinants. Their conception of personality emphasized the organization of intergrative processes of the brain to carry out certain functions: tension reduction, self-expression, reduction of conflicts by scheduling time and priorities and by social conformity and identification, and reduction of aspiration tensions. In short, they said, "personality operates to reduce 'dissatisfaction' and to heighten and extend 'satisfaction.' . . . The chief over-all function of personality, then, is to create a design for living which permits the periodic and harmonious appeasement of most of its needs as well as gradual progressions towards distant goals" (pp. 31-32).

The validity of these four factors as being important in personality formation is well documented. The fact that constitutional factors, genetic or nongenetic, are important in behavior development is reemphasized in recent statements by Garn (1966) with respect to stature; by the Scheibels (1964) in reference to neural substrates of postnatal development; and by McClearn (1964) concerning genetics and behavior development. McClearn discussed (pp. 472-473) the "unique and unrepeatable" quality of each human being and the fact that genotype and environment interact in development, a point emphasized by Kluckholn and Murray (1948).

Group membership as an important determinant of personality is illustrated by the review of Inkeles and Levinson (1969) in a discussion of "national character" and modal personality in sociocultural systems. These writers also referred to the influence of roles, as have Sarbin and Allen (1969)—especially in speaking of "self-role congruence" and "role enactment and social identity"— and also Biddle and Thomas (1966).

Such factors as sex, age, birth order, race, social class, and interpersonal relations within the family combine variously to create situations and other environmental and historical circumstances of learning which also affect personality development. These are illustrated by the work of Bandura and Walters (1963) and by the reviews of Becker (1964) and Clausen (1966). Moreover, the *interaction* of these factors, differentially perceived as they are by individuals, also influences the basic nature of personality. As Mussen has said, "All these forces are interwoven— operating, interacting, and affecting personality development concurrently" (1963, p. 58).

If all of these are determinants of personality development, there may well be grounds for challenging the notion of stability in adulthood, since it would follow that changes in these determinants would change personality.

Certainly, in the adult years there are constitutional changes: with advancing age, men and women typically become less strong and quick of movement and more prone to some forms of disease.

Certainly, there are changes in group membership: the adult moves from the family of his parents to one he creates himself. Children arrive, grow up, and leave the family scene; and eventually the adult may be widowed.

Certainly there are changes in the adult's roles: he moves from the role of student to worker, bachelor to husband, and later, from worker to retiree.

Also, his living situation may be altered: he may go off to new lands, to new activities with new people of his own choosing, and he may establish himself in a home quite different from that of his childhood or in an occupation quite unlike that of his parents.

These kinds of changes during adulthood, while not nearly so well documented as those occurring during childhood and adolescence, are described in some theoretical statements and reports of empirical studies. Such writers as Strehler (1962) and Birren, Butler, Greenhouse, Sokoloff, and Yarrow (1963) have given attention to the relation of age to biological characteristics. Investigators such as Cumming and Henry (1961), Lidz (1968), Neugarten and associates (1964), Perlman (1968), Sanford (1966), White (1966), and Williams and Wirths (1965) have been con-

cerned with social role, life style, and other changes or differences
with age in adulthood in relation to personality.

A conclusion from these statements might be that there are
many changes in the adult years in what Kluckhohn and Murray
call the determinants of personality. We would agree with Kuhlen:

> Age is *time* in which other things of importance happen.
> Among the important "other things" are: biological
> changes; changes in cognitive abilities; changes in habit
> strengths (flexibilities, rigidities); changes in patterns of
> reward, threat, punishment, opportunity, deprivation,
> training schedules, the latter tending to be culturally
> age-graded; and changes in motivation (Kuhlen, 1964, p.
> 554).

We would add the fact that time also brings societal, environmental, and situational changes that surely carry the potential for
important impact upon the social aspects of personality during
adulthood (Becker, 1964).

The assumption that "the major elements" of adult personality are laid down in childhood, so that adult personality can be
predicted from the study of child rearing and child personality, is
"overly simple" and "restrictive," according to Inkeles and
Levinson. They have said that this model of thinking "leads to the
neglect both of postchildhood changes in personality and of the
influence of sociocultural factors on personality development in
middle childhood, adolescence, and various periods of adult life"
(1969, p. 467). The view that personality formation in early
childhood is "basic" to adult personality places undue and
disproportional emphasis on early life, these writers believed, since
childhood simply provides a foundation or structural framework
for the personality of adulthood. Further, they believed that the
manifest *forms* of personality functioning may differ in adult life
from those in childhood, while the processes or typical mechanisms remain quite similar.

Continual Change During Adulthood

If these conceptions of the formation of personality are
correct, then personality may well be forming and re-forming
throughout all the adult years (Bromley, 1966, p. 77, 95). We

emphasize that such change or stability is *relative*. When changes in behavior and growth during childhood and adolescence are compared to those occurring in adulthood, the latter period does seem to be much more stable. In fact, common expressions about the "storm and stress" of youth and of "settling down" as they become adults emphasize that adult life is relatively quiet. We do not believe, however, that this means that change cannot or does not take place in the adult years.

In the middle and later portions of adult life, changes do occur in the ways in which individuals perceive themselves, their past experiences, and the time yet available to them. In middle-aged persons, Neugarten (1968, 1969) has observed

> the heightened importance of introspection in the mental life of middle-aged persons: the stocktaking, the increased reflection, and above all, the structuring and restructuring of experience—that is, the processing of new information in the light of experience; the use of this knowledge and expertise for the achievement of desired ends; the handing over to others or guarding for oneself the fruits of one's experience (1968, p. 139).

That this period in life is marked by changing problems of identity, "generativity," and "integrity" has been maintained by Erikson (1950) and elaborated on by Peck (1956). In sum, these views hardly emphasize the static nature of personality in adult life!

Restricted Opportunities for Change

There is another side to the story, however: the events that occur over the duration of time limit one's freedom to change many aspects of himself and his overt behavior. The choices made as one grows up and grows older do cut off opportunities for later choices. As Kuhlen has observed, "A person tends to get 'locked in' particular circumstances as he marries, has children, invests in property, accumulates training and seniority" (1964, p. 214). In short, there comes, from the sheer circumstances of a person's life, a "point of no return"—a situation Kuhlen saw as an age-related frustration in the face of motivational change. Nevertheless, we would argue that belief in such decreased freedom to change does not require us to think that change is impossible, particularly in the more "inner" or "internal" aspects of personality and adjustment.

Maintenance and Prevention of Decline

In the latter part of the life span the processes of formation and re-formation might be considered elements of a preventive or personal maintenance process in relation to the "natural" decline that is said to occur with age. Some writers have, in fact, defined aging simply in terms of downward changes following a period of relative stability (Anderson, 1964, p. 12). An older man or woman may have to "fight" harder simply to maintain stability in the face of the biological deficit known to be a common aspect of aging. Failure to be able to make at least minimal adaptation and changes, however, may lead to the end of survival, with one failure leading to another and still another, in a fashion that reverses the sequence of successes outlined by developmental task theorists (Havighurst, 1953, p. 2).

Utility of Concept of Continuity

Undoubtedly the commonsense notion that there is little personality change in adulthood is an important assumption of everyday social interaction. Kelly referred to this in his presidential address to the American Psychological Association:

> Perhaps because of the need to believe in consistency of one's self from moment to moment and from year to year, we tend to infer an unwarranted degree of consistency in others. Some consistency is indeed necessary for social intercourse, and it is likely that, as a matter of convenience in remembering and dealing with our associates, we utilize stereotypy to a considerable degree and thus tend to infer greater consistency in others than may be the case (Kelly, 1955, p. 659).

Continuity and Change in Personality Theories

In most theories of personality it is also widely accepted that the individual's unique personality is consistent and sustained over time. As Kelly said:

> Whether one's thinking about these matters stems from the writings of William James or that of other psychological theorists, the answer is likely to be the same; on perhaps no other major issue do widely variant psychological theories lead to such congruent predictions. Whether one is an extreme hereditarian, an environmentalist, a constitutionalist, or an orthodox psychoanalyst, he is not likely to anticipate major changes in personality after the first few years of life (Kelly, 1955, p. 659).

In their review of personality theories, Hall and Lindzey (1970) examined the extent to which theorists emphasized the continuity or lack of continuity of development from childhood to adulthood and "the relative independence of the functioning adult from the events of childhood and infancy." These authors commented that not all theorists displayed interest in the process of development as "a continuous process to be represented in terms of a single set of theoretical principles" (p. 587). Their analysis showed that little or no concern was given by any theory, except Carl Jung's "analytic theory," to change that might occur in the adult years. They detailed Jung's view as follows:

> When an individual reaches the late thirties or early forties a radical transvaluation occurs. Youthful interests and pursuits lose their value and are replaced by new interests which are more cultural and less biological. The middle-aged person becomes more introverted and less impulsive. Wisdom and sagacity take the place of physical and mental vigor. His values are sublimated in social, religious, civic, and philosophical symbols. He is transformed into a spiritual man.
> This transition is the most decisive event in a person's life. It is also one of the most hazardous because if anything goes amiss during the transference of energy the personality may become permanently crippled. . . . Jung has had a great deal of success treating middle-aged people whose energies have failed to find satisfying outlets (Hall and Lindzey, 1970, pp. 99-100).

Another theoretical approach to personality development and

change over the adult years was that made by Neugarten (1964, 1966, 1968). She called for a personality theory which will encompass the life cycle—one which will emphasize "the ego or executive functions of the personality; one which will help account for the growth and maintenance of cognitive competence and creativity, one that will help explain the conscious use of past experience" (1968, p. 147). She warned against applying to the adult years the biological model of growth and development, with the concepts of increasing differentiation and integration and an end-point toward which change is directed, and said, "Psychologists should proceed cautiously in assuming the same intimate relationships between biological and psychological phenomena in adulthood that hold true in childhood" (p. 142). In addition, Neugarten emphasized the "pervasive quality" of age-norms influencing the psychology of adulthood, indicating that the norms about the timing of life events provide "some of the most powerful cues to adult personality" (p. 144).

Need for Empirical Data

We think it important to provide empirical data that bear on the question of the extent to which the adult does modify his personality and adjustment pattern, especially during the later years of life. How an *adult* "mobilizes," "mediates," "uses," and "maintains" his personality and adjustment pattern is of significance in order to expand theories of personality and behavior so they can account for the variations occurring throughout the course of life. How the varying environment forces change in the adult's behavior needs to be known. It is also important that action programs dealing with problems of health, employment, retirement, housing, or whatever, be based upon knowledge of what continuity occurs or does not occur over the latter part of the life cycle. It is our hope to contribute to such knowledge. These findings are presented in Chapter 3.

SURVIVAL

Aging itself is a process by which selected members of the species continue to live while others do not. Hence, any study of change over time must inquire into the nature of those individuals who survive the years. This is more than a question of the characteristics of surviving subjects or samples of persons, for such inquiry pertains most broadly to the nature of evolution. Charles Darwin, who spent a lifetime amassing evidence on this topic, noted:

As many more individuals of each species are born than can possibly survive; and as, consequently, there is a frequently recurring struggle for existence, it follows that any being, if it vary however slightly in any manner profitable to itself, under the complex and sometimes varying conditions of life, will have a better chance of surviving, and thus be naturally selected. From the strong principle of inheritance, any selected variety will tend to propagate its new and modified form (Darwin, 1859, p. 23).

In our study of continuity and change, we noted the rapid attrition of the subjects in a short period of time. Such attrition was mostly by death. The question arose, then, of how well our surviving population of older adults represented the total group of which they were once a part. Birren has stated:

Persons at about age 65-70 represent only about half of their population at birth. If death occurs randomly, a systematic bias in survivors would not exist, but, since they do not all die in accidents, there is the possibility of a considerable selection process in the survivors of the birth population. Survivors might be, for example, taller or shorter, brighter or duller, happier or unhappier than their non-surviving cohorts. . . . If earlier measurements on the subjects are available, we may compare the present sample retrospectively with the "total" population alive at an earlier date. The principle to be stressed is that studies of aging yield data on survivors of a larger earlier population which is susceptible to selective mortality (Birren, 1959a, p. 30).

Continuing to live or to escape death may be a purely biological phenomenon, and considerable attention is regularly given to accumulating data on mortality trends and comparing them according to age, sex, and cause of death (U.S. Department of Health, Education, and Welfare, 1966). For example, in 1968 persons aged 70 living in the United States could expect to live an additional 11.6 years on the average, and such persons had an annual mortality rate of 39.5 per 1,000 (Metropolitan Life Insurance Company, 1969, p. 8). Such rates differ, of course, by sex; and rates of death from diseases of the heart, for example, are considerably higher than those from cancer and other causes (U.S. Department of Health, Education, and Welfare, 1966).

Some investigators, however, have been concerned with nonbiological variables such as education and income in relation to mortality. For example, Kitagawa and Hauser (1968) have shown that for white females 65 and over in the United States the mortality rate of major cardiovascular-renal diseases for those with less than eight years of school was 1.71 times the rate of those with one or more years of college. The same was not true for males (1968, p. 336). However, in 15 of the 18 causes of death reported for males, and in 14 of the 17 reported for females, there was an inverse relationship with education (p. 348).

In the current study there was concern for some of the nonbiological factors relating to survival. How do survivors over a period of years in old age differ from nonsurvivors on certain social and psychological variables? Findings from this part of the investigation are presented in Chapter 4.

AGING IN A SMALL COMMUNITY SETTING

In our study, we decided to concentrate on the aging of "normal" adults living in their natural surroundings. We wanted a community that was itself quite stable and was also the "hometown" of most of the older residents. The population we sought, then, should consist of individuals living and functioning as members of a long-established community. Most of them, probably, would be residing in their own homes, often in locations where they had lived for many years. Most would be living more or less independently; some would be working and some would be "retired." Some would be living with families, some would be widowed, and some would doubtless be single and living alone. Since we were seeking a "representative" study group on such variables as well as on personality and adjustment, we believed it necessary to seek all available subjects in the selected area.

This kind of subject population could be contrasted with an institutionalized one in which the subjects might have been more available and accessible. Residents of a home for the aged, for example, might have been studied, but they represent a highly selected population. Perhaps, seeking volunteers in one way or another would have assured a more cooperative study group, especially desirable in a study that extended over a period of years, but we were not intending, either, to study the adjustment of volunteers.

Aside from our concern with the kinds of older individuals who were to appear in our study population, we were also interested in the nature of the *community* in which they lived. Individuals are, of course, affected by the kind of community in which they live, and they, in turn, can to some degree have an effect on the community. Over the course of the research we gained some impressions about the study community as a place in which to live and age. These observations are presented in Chapter 5, along with data about how the study community viewed its aged.

One further matter relates to the selection of our study community. We wished to compare methods commonly used by psychologists in personality research with assessments made by the lay associates of individual subjects in the community. Therefore, we sought a community in which residents knew each other reasonably well. The likelihood of this happening was greatest in a small and stable rural community, which in the United States typically has a fairly large proportion of older persons. As an environment for older persons, this type of setting needs study.

The locale finally selected for the research was a Pennsylvania village of 1,000 persons and the surrounding township of another 1,000 persons: "Pennsboro" and "Green Township." This community is the center of an agricultural area and is quite typical of rural and rural nonfarm areas in Pennsylvania. About 10 percent of the population was aged 65 and over, and all individuals in the area in this age group were listed as potential subjects for the study.

OBJECTIVES OF THE RESEARCH

The purpose of the research was to investigate some behavioral processes of aging by studying consistency of personality and adjustment in old age, as well as the problem of survivorship. Aging was to be viewed developmentally, as change over time, in contrast to differences between age groups.

Furthermore, aging persons were to be studied in their "natural habitats"—in their own homes in the community in which most of them had lived most of their lives. For this study, personality and adjustment were defined in terms of both their "inner" (personal) and "outer" (social) aspects.

The specific aims of the investigation were:

1. To determine the consistency or change in personality and adjustment of older adults over time and to learn what factors are related to consistency or change. These findings are presented in Chapter 3.

2. To study the problem of survivorship by analyzing differences between survivors in order to show some social-psychological correlates of survival. These findings are given in Chapter 4.

3. To investigate the social norms and expectations for the behavior of older persons in order to learn how a small community regards its aged members. Such information was intended to provide the opportunity for certain appraisals of the community as a place to live and age. The results of this analysis are presented in Chapter 5.

We shall now describe the nature of the study community, the initiation of the investigation, and some characteristics of the participating subjects.

Chapter 2

The Research Setting and the Study Populations

THE HISTORICAL SETTING

The historical setting for the present investigation was in the early part of the 1950's, not long after a first national conference on the aging and the aged indicated the dearth of knowledge that scientists and practitioners had of them. The Gerontological Society was in its infancy or early childhood, and other professional circles were beginning to form for purposes of increasing knowledge and professional proficiency in order to cope with some of the problems on the horizons. Governmentally sponsored research on aging was in its early stages of development. There was increasing interest in gerontology, in training and in research, but much of its development as a field of study, related to whatever discipline, was yet to occur.

OBSERVATIONS ON GERONTOLOGY

As we began to think about our own contribution to research in gerontology, we made several observations of the psychological and social sciences in relation to the aging. First, important work was being carried out in laboratories to extend the knowledge of behavioral processes to old age. Usually such work involved previously defined variables, for which experimental operations were readily available. While findings from these studies did extend knowledge of behavior under prescribed circumstances, they generally appeared to have remote value in solving the *problems* confronting people as they grew older. Second, investigations typically compared the young and the old, variously delineated, and implied that they were studying processes of aging. Strictly speaking, however, they recognized that cross-sectional designs could show only age differences and not age changes.

A third observation was that most studies of the aged dealt with special groups by virtue of their being "available": residents of old age homes, patients in convalescent facilities, retired school teachers or YMCA secretaries, or other highly selected groups. Further, subjects were often the volunteers or the willing participants who selected themselves or were selected by others for the studies, with relatively little reference to their representativeness of the larger group.

These statements seem valid as descriptive of the research being done on aging as we began our project. They cannot, however, be considered indictments of the scientists of the time. In fact, when the scientific knowledge of aging up to those dates was compiled and placed in context, it was impressive (Birren, 1959b; Burgess, 1960; Cowdry, 1939; Shock, 1951, 1957, 1963; Tibbitts, 1960).

The observations we had made guided our own efforts to contribute to the field. They told us that we might usefully strike out to study the changes that take place in the ways in which ordinary older persons, residing in their own homes in a given community, live and adjust over a period of several years. Since we recognized that there was something special about those who were able to live to old age, we wanted to study the selective nature of the aging process, as well as explore the relationships between individual behavior and the community environment. In our research we intended to study natural phenomena, with as little interference or interruption from outside forces as possible; because of this orientation, we were guarded in our formal and informal approaches to individuals in the study community. While we did hope to learn something useful about the mental health of older adults, we did not intend to intervene in our subjects' lives. If our procedures made our subjects more self-conscious or "unnatural" about their lives (and we do not believe they did), this was never our desire.

The kind of study we were contemplating made it clear that a community-field approach was required. We turned our attention to the selection of a setting that would meet these objectives.

CRITERIA FOR SELECTION OF A COMMUNITY

In selecting a natural setting for our longitudinal research with older people, several criteria were considered. In the first place, we needed a fairly stable community, without heavy influx or out-migration of either the older people themselves or other community members. This also meant that the community would have to be sufficiently large for enough older people to be present to allow for the natural attrition of the older subjects without seriously reducing the size for analyses. At the same time, the community would have to be small enough so that older persons could be known by others, and also small enough so that the total group of older people—and not simply a sample of them—could be followed over time (Willits, Crider, and Bealer, 1969). We did not, however, want to study a retirees' community.

In addition, we felt that the community should be fairly typical of other small communities, being neither richer nor poorer than many others nor having some special characteristic or structure that dominated it. It should be a relatively independent community with a life of its own, we decided, one outside the shadow of a large city or a major institution, such as a university or industrial concern.

A further thought was related to our general concern with the mental health of older persons: we wanted certain types of "mental health services" available to the study population. We wanted a small community, but not one so isolated or backward that commonly accepted psychiatric and "social services," through clinics or hospitals, would not be available. Part of our interest, in fact, was in how such services were perceived and used.

Practicality dictated that we locate a community within a reasonable distance from the university where we worked, so that field work could be carried out conveniently and effectively, but it could not be one that had been "over-researched" by previous field studies. And, of course, we wanted a community in which we could be confident that we would receive a cooperative welcome in our repeated visits over the years.

These criteria indicated that a real "community" was the desired setting for the study—a community in the traditional sense of a people living in a limited geographical area who engage in a common social life. This is probably best typified by a rural community (see Crider, 1969), and such an area was selected. As we considered the problem of community selection more carefully, another important factor became clear. The rural elderly exist in substantial numbers in the United States. In 1960, for example, they numbered over five million, or one-third of all those aged 65 and over. One government report said, "This is not an insignificant statistic since an overall shortage of medical facilities and personnel and other community programs is most frequently present in the rural areas of the Nation" (U.S. Senate Special Committee on Aging, 1961, p. 21). We deemed it quite appropriate, therefore, that the study be carried out in such a rural community setting.

CHARACTERISTICS OF THE SELECTED COMMUNITY

The community that most closely met the criteria and was, therefore, selected as a setting for the study was a rural community located in central Pennsylvania, within a driving distance of one and a half hours from the main campus of the university where the authors worked. The initial contact was made at a state professional meeting with a professional person in the area, followed by a review of demographic data to determine how typical or atypical the community was. Additional contact with the county agent through the university's Agricultural Extension Service verified earlier reports and confirmed the preliminary judgment about the area as the locale for our research. As we shall explain later, these prefatory appraisals were to be tested by later considerations, but let us now describe the community finally settled upon.

The area to be studied consisted of a village (borough, in Pennsylvania parlance), which was the county seat, and the surrounding township. We have given these places fictitious names: the village is "Pennsboro," surrounded by "Green Township," in "Liberty County." In 1950, five years before we began the study, the population of Pennsboro was about 1,000; that of Green Township, another 1,000. As such, the village was classified by the Census Bureau as rural nonfarm, and the township as both rural nonfarm and rural farm. Liberty County's population was approximately 25,000 in 1950, when almost two-thirds were rural nonfarm, less than one-third rural farm, and about one-twelfth urban residents. These proportions differed considerably from the state as a whole: in 1950, 70.5 percent of Pennsylvania was urban, 22.8 percent was rural nonfarm, and 6.7 percent was rural farm. Thus, our study population was selected from an area that is largely rural and is unlike the rest of the Commonwealth in this respect (Lansing, 1956).

On the basis of data comparing Liberty County with Pennsylvania as a whole, the following general statements (Lansing, 1956, p. 28) show the similarities and differences:

1. Liberty County is unlike Pennsylvania in that it is largely rural, while the state is chiefly urban.

2. The county is largely native white and has a greater proportion in this category than the state.

3. The county and the state are similar with regard to marital status, labor force participation, and in-migration.

4. The average size of families in Liberty County is a little larger than that in the state as a whole.

5. The population of Liberty County has, according to median figures, approximately $600 less annual income per family than is true of families in the rest of the state. They are somewhat less well educated than those in the state as a whole.

6. Proportionally more people live in one-dwelling detached structures in the county than in the state. The homes in the county are worth less and, proportionally, more of them lack modern conveniences.

7. A larger percentage of residents in Liberty County own their own homes, as compared with the state as a whole.

8. Liberty County spends more money per capita on education than the average for the state. The value of school property per pupil enrolled and the median salary of classroom teachers are less than those for the state. The proportion of teachers holding advanced degrees is lower than for the state, but a higher proportion of teachers are men.

9. A slightly larger proportion of the farms in the county are owned by the operator, as compared with the average in the state as a whole.

10. The average value of farm products sold per farm in the county is less than for the state.

11. The farms in Liberty County are worth about one-third less per farm and about one-half less per acre than those in Pennsylvania generally.

12. The county produces a slightly lower average yield per acre of selected farm produce.

The 1950 census data on age showed that of the population of the state, 8.4 percent—and of Liberty County, just over 9 percent—were 65 years old and over (U.S. Bureau of the Census, 1952). In Pennsboro, however, almost 12 percent were in this age group, of whom 58 percent were women. A considerable proportion of the older population of the borough consisted of retired farmers and their wives or widows, professional and small business men and women, and persons associated with county governmental activities.

DESCRIPTION OF THE SETTING

The Area

Pennsboro is in the center of Green Township in an area considered one of the state's loveliest in natural beauty. Several streams and a major river pass through the county, affording attractive spots for hunting and fishing. Homes in the countryside are nestled amongst softly rolling and fishing. Homes in the countryside are nestled amonst softly rolling hills or spread in valleys, which in spring and early summer are green with wheat, oats, hay, alfalfa, and corn. Dairy farmers boast large barns and, oftentimes, fine Guernsey herds. Almost all families in the countryside, and many in Pennsboro, "put out" a large garden and rely on it to produce a considerable portion of their food supply. Most residents take pride in how their houses and yards look and in how well their gardens fill their larders.

Several miles away lies another small town not much larger than Pennsboro, and within about a half-hour's drive one can reach two medium-sized cities that provide sources of employment to some Pennsboro residents. Those who want outside shopping, professional consultation, or special recreational or cultural activities not available in Pennsboro can usually find them in those two cities if they have their own transportation to get there. When we began the study, buses went through Pennsboro; later, no public transportation was available in the research area.

Pennsboro

In the center of Pennsboro is a town square, dominated by a monument dedicated to those who gave their lives in the War between the States. The two major streets, Main Street and Church Street, cross at the square. The Liberty County Courthouse, with its red brick walls and white shuttered windows, towers over one corner, as it has for almost a century. On another corner is a two-story building said to be constructed of log, now covered with white clapboard, which once housed overnight guests en route overland to connecting points of the historic Pennsylvania canal and "rail" system. The public lawns nearby are neatly kept, and the huge maple trees lend their shade to those who sit on the benches beside the walks.

Although national chain stores have now taken over the main local grocery and drugstore, and the bank is now a branch of one in the city, they continue their activities in the old locations on the square. Shopping malls and suburban-type supermarkets are not a part of the way of life in Liberty County. The business buildings are, for the most part, well maintained. Governmental officers were located above stores until they were relocated in a courthouse annex; some of these rooms were converted into apartments in which some of the few apartment dwellers now live.

A mill and a feed store are down the hill on Church Street, a block or two beyond two of the Protestant churches. In a building that formerly housed a Protestant congregation, a branch of the County Library has recently been established. On two of the roads leading from town, agricultural machinery dealers have set up shop, and near one of them a new Catholic Church has been built, served by a priest who comes out from the city. Up the hill in a plot set back from the road is the community's only cemetery. Not far away in new, ranch-type houses (in a section jokingly referred to by some as "Mortgage Row") live several younger families, headed by business or professional people. Only one of our older subjects lived there; he made his home with his daughter and her family. New elementary and secondary schools are not far away.

During the summer the benches on the square are often occupied by some of the older men of the community, and occasionally our interviews were held there. There were few other public places to meet; for instance, there is no tavern in Pennsboro. The only tavern, about a mile outside of town, is largely frequented by a younger crowd of workingmen.

Daily Life

The usual day in Pennsboro begins a little before nine o'clock, when children can be seen on their way to school (some are bussed

in from outlying districts). Businesses begin to open and merchants take the opportunity to attend to extra chores around their
establishments, sweeping the front walks or loading in new stock.

The post office begins "putting up" its mail around ten, if the
mail truck arrives on time, and people come in to watch their
postal boxes being filled and to chat. Local news is exchanged, and
the postmaster and his assistant, through discreet listeners and
reporters, are kept informed of the whereabouts and "goings on"
of nearly everyone in the community.

The Newspaper

A block away, on a side street, the weekly newspaper is
published. Its columns carry county news sent in by correspon-
dents in outlying communities, as well as county legal notices.
Many photographs add interest. At county election time the pages
are filled with reports of political activities. Editorials generally
pertain to local affairs or to state matters that have local
implications.

The Homes

Most houses in the area are two-story dwellings of frame,
native stone, or brick; those in Pennsboro generally have a small
front yard and porch, with space in the back or on the side for a
vegetable and flower garden. Houses located on Main Street are
built next to the sidewalk, providing a large backyard. Sheds and
barns to the rear of older properties sometimes have a few
chickens inside, along with the family car and gardening equipment. Most dwellings are painted white. Public opinion as well as
the pride of the residents is relied upon to assure that the neatness
and attractiveness of the community are maintained.

Houses typically contain a living room, dining room, kitchen,
and pantry downstairs, and two or three bedrooms and a bath
upstairs. Virtually all homes have indoor plumbing and electricity
and contain most modern applicances, although sometimes, in
addition to a modern stove, older residents keep a wood range in
the kitchen. Most homes are heated by coal or oil furnaces or oil
room heaters. Radios and television sets are possessed by nearly
everyone.

LIAISON AND LAUNCHING

During the winter and spring of 1955, while final plans for the project were being laid, we proceeded to build liaison with the study community. Since the success of this portion of the work was crucial for the entire investigation, the importance of our taking time at this point to establish wide contact in the community cannot be overestimated.

Purposes

This phase had three purposes:

1. To ascertain, through further contacts with community leaders, whether the community would respond favorably to our proposed field study. The intent was to study the matter thoroughly in order to reaffirm the fact that there were no important reasons why we should not proceed with the field study.

2. To establish *ourselves*—vis-a-vis community leaders and officials, professional people, and other—as competent, responsible, and trustworthy professional persons.

3. To disseminate knowledge about the purposes of the study to particular community members who might inform others concerning the project and interpret it or the investigators' intentions as legitimate and worthy. We thought that this would best come from community members informally and only if they themselves felt it necessary or desirable in the community. We did not ask directly for assistance in this, but we learned later that some ministers had spontaneously mentioned the study positively to their congregations.

Contacts with Leaders

Rather early in our liaison work one of us volunteered to talk to meetings of the men's service club and of a similar women's group. This move was followed promptly by an invitation to talk to a special dinner meeting of the two groups, husbands and wives included, in the spring of 1955. The topic dealt with aging and mental health. The need for knowledge on the subject was emphasized, and we indicated that if all went according to plan we would be returning to Pennsboro and Green Township to conduct a survey on the matter. The meeting was held at a church, and a capacity crowd attended, including quite a number of older residents of Liberty County. The interest was keen, as we recall, and many commented, as the meeting adjourned, that we had come to the right place if we wanted to study old people! "There are plenty of them around here, and they like it here!" we were told. The reception was warm and friendly, and we decided to proceed.

Many community leaders and officials were thus informally contacted about the study. As a follow-up we personally contacted the sheriff, all ministers, county officials, and physicians, as well as county school, and public assistance officials. We visited the postmaster, the high school principal, the funeral director, and the local newspaper publisher. The staff of the university's Agricultural and Home Economics Extension Office in Liberty County was especially helpful; their keen knowledge of the people and of the area was most useful to us in this liaison phase. When we called upon each of these persons we gave them a copy of a news release that was simultaneously being sent to the radio and television stations and to the newspapers serving the area. A copy of a press release, typical of those released throughout the study, is included here as Appendix A.

Community Consultants

During this phase of the work, we were ably assisted by several consultants—professional and lay persons in the community, who knew it well and gave us invaluable advice on a myriad of practical matters. They continued throughout the years of the study to offer encouragement and judgment concerning our work. They cannot be mentioned by name, but we are certain that any success achieved by the project was in large measure due to their wisdom and understanding.

Our research plan called for a community-wide survey and for later return calls to interview all the older persons. Let us turn to an explanation of the first of these.

PROCEDURES AND SUBJECTS
OF THE COMMUNITY SURVEY

Objectives

Early in the summer of 1955 we began our first period of data collection by means of a community-wide survey. This phase of the work had three objectives:

1. To locate each older person in the area for the subsequent phases of the project, we needed to take a complete "census" of each household in the community (Appendix B). One adult in each household was to be asked to give his name and address, and to indicate whether he owned or rented his home, and the length of time he had lived in the community. The names of all the other occupants in the household, their relationship to one another, and information about their ages, educational status, and occupation were to be obtained.

2. To obtain data concerning the social norms for older people held by residents of the community, we sought knowledge about expectations for older persons with reference to work and retirement, family relationships, community participation, and ways of solving personal problems. Social norms are defined as the standards by which social behavior is approved or disapproved, and these were intended to describe the guides and regulations of behavior of individual older persons in the community.

3. To determine which older individuals the residents of the community viewed as being well-adjusted or poorly adjusted with respect to the social norms, so that we could identify such individuals who by reputation stood out positively or negatively in reference to group norms.

The Interview Schedule

For this first phase of the project an interview schedule (Appendix C) was organized around problems of older persons: retirement, living arrangements, social relationships, community participation, personal problems, and ways in which these might be solved. Several open-ended questions were used—for example, "What do you think are the best living arrangements for an older person?" A number of anecdotal questions were used—for example, "Because she is pretty lonesome after the death of her husband, Mrs. Sayles rented out her own home and moved in with her married daughter. What do you think of this?" And: "Bill Brown was in good health, but since he had saved enough money to retire, he sold out to his son and he and his wife moved away. What do you think about this?" The replies furnished data concerning social norms for old people in the area.

Respondents were also asked to name older residents whom they thought had worked out good living arrangements or had gotten along well with members of their family, etc. These answers provided reputation ratings for older persons in the community.

The Interviewing

A team of seven interviewers, under the direction of a field supervisor, canvassed the 540 households in the community. In each case they tried to speak with the head of the household if he or she was at home. Otherwise an adult member of the household was interviewed, and often it was the housewife. Persons who refused an interview with one worker were called on by another. In this way, each person was given at least two, and often more, opportunities to participate. If he refused, the interviewer tried to obtain the basic data about the persons in the household. It was hoped that a complete census would thus be obtained, and where the basic information could not be obtained directly, the interviewer tried to secure it from a neighbor.

Interview schedules were completed for an adult in 487 households, or 90.2 percent of the 540 known households. An additional 24 persons (4.4 percent) gave partial information, 10 (1.9 percent) refused altogether, and persons in 19 living units (3.5 percent) were not able to be contacted directly despite repeated visits. It is believed, however, that virtually every person aged 65 or over was located in the survey.

The Participants

Of the 487 interviewees, 102 were men and 385 were women. Background information concerning them was tabulated. Such facts are pertinent to interpreting the normative data about expectations for older persons. Male informants tended to be somewhat older than the women informants: the median age was 59.1 for men compared to 49.2 for women. On the whole, women interviewees had had more years of schooling than the men: 27 percent of the women and 13 percent of the men had graduated from high school; 20 percent of the women and 15 percent of the men had had some college. About one-half of the respondents were members of families where the wage earner was (or before death or retirement had been) in a middle-status occupation. Eighty percent of the interviewees had lived in the community over five years. More men than women had older persons living in the family, and the great majority of both men and women were married and living with their spouses.

The interviewer read the statements of activities to each participant; he wrote all comments, as nearly as possible in the words of the respondent, on the schedule. The interviews averaged about one hour in length. At the completion, the research worker thanked him for his cooperation and gave him a short mimeographed statement explaining the study and giving an address where he could obtain more information if he wished to do so.

Responses from these 487 persons who had talked about the problems of older people became the basis for determining the social norms of the community. To show how closely older persons agreed with the community norms, an Opinion Conformity Scale was devised for use with them; this scale will be described in Chapter 3. The social norms are discussed in Chapter 5.

THE OLDER SUBJECTS

The complete house-to-house survey in 1955 located 205 persons *64* years of age or over then living in Pennsboro and Green Township; 80 of them were men and 125 were women. The plan of the research involved interviewing and assessing this total group of older persons over the subsequent years of the study.

In 1956, one year after the area-wide "census" had been taken, 29 persons aged 65 and over had died or moved away, and 176 were still living and in the area. Using our procedures for assessing personality and adjustment, we were able to interview 146 individuals, 59 men and 87 women, or 83 percent of the eligible subjects.

In 1962, after a period of six years, 95 older persons who were part of the original group of subjects were still living and in the area. Of these, 81 persons (24 men and 47 women) were interviewed, 71 for the second time (Davidson, 1963).

By 1965, of the original group of subjects, 70 persons were living and still in the area. Interviews were held with 53 of these persons, 19 men and 34 women.

Longitudinal Subjects

Data on 17 men and 29 women, a total of 46, were available from these three waves of interviewing and testing over the nine-year period. Longitudinal analyses could be made for these people, and we called them our "longitudinal subjects." How much they differed from the original groups of subjects interviewed and tested in 1956 was a question we wanted to answer in thinking about participation versus nonparticipation in community studies, as well as in thinking about the nature of survivors versus nonsurvivors (Chapter 4).

To help us in determining the representativeness of our longitudinal subjects, we used a chi-square analysis comparing the longitudinal subjects with those who, for whatever reason—death, departure from the community, illness, or refusal—did not participate in our later follow-ups. These findings are presented in Table 1. Apparently, participation for men was somewhat different than for women, and except on the variable of occupational status, the male participants in the longitudinal group were representative of the original interviewee population. The 17 longitudinal male subjects included a significantly more-than-expected number of men from the upper-status occupational categories. (See the descriptive tables in Chapter 3.)

The women longitudinal subjects are *over*-represented with "younger" ones and with those who rated their health "good" or "excellent" in 1956. Significantly more of them than expected by chance had high scores on the Activity Inventory, Attitude Inventory, and Judge's Rating, measures with a definite activity dimension (Britton, 1962). In addition, by comparison, the longitudinal women significantly often had the high scores on the Opinion Conformity Scale, indicating their tendency to conform to community norms more than those women in the 1956 interview population who did not become longitudinal subjects.

TABLE 1

Chi-Square Values for Factors Comparing Longitudinal
Subjects with Other 1956 Interviewees, by Sex

Factor	Men	Women
Age	1.25	6.46*
Marital status	1.51	.24
Living arrangements	1.52	.10
Education	3.39	.15
Occupation of family wage earner	3.96*	2.96
Health self-rating	.00	11.60*
Activity Inventory	2.50	7.25*
Attitude Inventory	2.49	8.25*
Judge's Rating	1.23	10.10*
Personal Relations and Sociability Scale	.81	2.60
Thematic Apperception Test	.01	.25
Opinion Conformity Scale	.21	8.29*
Reputation Rating	.00	.99
Interviewer's Rating	.02	2.85

*Significant at the 5 or less than 5 percent level; $df = 1$.

These findings about the representativeness of our longitudinal
study groups are, of course, related to our analyses of survivorship.
To be a longitudinal subject one must have survived, naturally, but
our emphasis here is upon how well in retrospect the longitudinal
subjects do represent the original subjects of which they were a
part. Like other longitudinal studies, we deal with a select
population, but this appears to be true much more for women
than for men. In Chapter 4 we will discuss the characteristics of
persons who survive the years, as well as of those who do not.

A sample of older persons received special attention in the
study by being subjects of evaluations by members of the
community. These persons, called the Q group, are described in
Chapter 5.

Summary

In this chapter we have sketched the historical setting for the
research. We set out the criteria for selecting a study community
and we described the particular community finally selected—

Pennsboro and the surrounding Green Township. We discussed how liaison was made with persons in the area and how the project was launched and carried out. In addition, we provided information about the participants in the normative survey of the research area and about the older residents and participants in the longitudinal study. We shall now examine and present findings about continuity and change in personality and adjustment for older persons.

Chapter 3

Continuity and Change
in Personality and Adjustment

THE QUESTIONS

In this section we shall proceed directly to two central questions of the research investigation:

1. How do personality and adjustment change over the latter part of the life span?
2. What personal and social factors are related to continuity and change?

These questions, and their answers, have theoretical significance to the study of personality development and change across the human life cycle. We have already referred to some of the conceptions of personality and its modification across the years of adulthood. These matters have importance, too, in many practical aspects of aging. How individuals and societies will attempt to control or to deal with changes occurring with age depends upon how "natural" or "normal" they view such changes. How much change one might expect to occur, and under what circumstances, also suggests ways of viewing the processes of aging and of seeing their potential for maintenance, decline, or even improvement. As Yarrow (1964) has said, "We must come to terms with the changing capacities of the individual, his changing relationship to his environment, and his changing roles at different developmental periods (p. 68). . . . A major research task is to identify the factors, environmental and organismic, underlying personality continuity and those that foster change" (p. 71).

The first question asked for a description of the changes, if any, which occur over a period in later maturity and old age. It represented an attempt to determine with whom, and when and how, and how much continuity or change occurs. In addition, however, we wished to learn, if we could, what events in individuals' lives, what circumstances in their surroundings, or what characteristics of their behavior were associated with continuity or change in this late period of the life span. These purposes are implicit in our second question, which was based upon the desire to be able to predict what kinds of individuals do or do not change and what factors apparently bear upon such change.

THE RESEARCH DESIGN

The research questions obviously involve the *processes* of development or aging, and they have the *passage of time* as their most basic dimension. An investigation involving the study of the same individuals over a considerable period of time—*a longitudinal design*—is called for by these questions. This design is in contrast to a cross-sectional design, in which individuals who have lived for differing lengths of time are studied.

The longitudinal method is seen as the basic method by which age changes can be studied (Birren, 1959, p. 20; Jones, 1960; Harris, 1963). In spite of repeated calls for longitudinal studies of development and aging, few seem to realize the pitfalls of these studies. While they may provide information on development and change over time, they do so for increasingly selective groups of subjects. The investigators must elicit and maintain cooperation with the subjects over time. In research with adults—and especially in the later years of adult life—investigators must also give attention to characteristics of individuals who survive the years and continue to be available to participate in the longitudinal research.

Additional problems of research design in the developmental and gerontological sciences include such issues as age versus generational differences, as well as practical matters of maintaining a research team for the duration of the project and the possibility of subjects gaining "practice" with repeated measurements (for example, Kessen, 1960; Anderson, 1964; see also Kodlin and Thompson, 1958, and Emmerick, 1969, for useful appraisals of longitudinal methodology).

Alternative models to the longitudinal design include Bell's "convergence" approach; this involves "combining the cross-sectional and longitudinal techniques in such a way that developmental changes for a long period may be estimated in a much shorter period" (1953, pp. 146-147) by "making limited remeasurements of cross-sectional groups so that temporally overlapping measurements of older and younger subjects are provided" (1954, p. 281). Schaie (1965) distinguished among three sources of developmental change: *cohort* differences (Woodruff, 1970), that is, differences between generations (for example, a 20-year-old in 1950 versus a 20-year-old in 1970); *time* differences, i.e., net changes within the environment (for example, assessment made in 1950 versus 1970); and *age* differences, that is, net age changes over time within the organism (for example, a 20-year-old assessed in 1950 and again as a 40-year-old in 1970). His "sequential design" is an attempt to provide an efficient means to enable age-cohort-time (age-genetic-cultural) variables to be differentiated (Schaie, 1967, 1971a, 1971b). Baltes (1968) reconceptualized Schaie's model in terms of only the components of age and cohort, since both depend in part upon time. The decision between whether to use a design with repeated (longitudinal) measurements or one with independent (cross-sectional) measurements depends, Baltes said, upon how sensitive the variables are to change over time and upon the investigator's desire to determine individual trends and control the effects of selective survival (p. 160). If the desire is to provide an analysis of individual trends (a paramount concern in the present study), a design with repeated measurements is necessary, Baltes noted; he referred to such a plan for data collection as an "age-sequential" or "time-lag" method (p. 165). In a discussion of statistical analysis of longitudinal data, Goldfarb (1960) called it "a method of repeated observations from a fixed sample."

In the present research, concern is with *continuity of individual behavior* over a considerable period of time in the later decades of life. Data obtained from and about older persons as segments of the population typically show a high incidence of illness and other problems among this age group, and the surviving and participating subjects do constitute an increasingly select population. Part of our research problem is to learn how select our longitudinal subjects really are. Only by obtaining data on how *individuals* maintain, decline, or improve their standing on whatever measure are we able to study the issues of continuity and change or the increasing selectivity of our study population.

George Bernard Shaw saw the need for longitudinal procedures when, in *Man and Superman*, one character observed that he hated to be treated as a boy when he was a man:

... to be treated as a boy was to be taken on the old footing. I had become a new person; and those who knew the old person laughed at me. The only man who behaved sensibly was my tailor: he took my measure anew every time he saw me, whilst all the rest went on with their old measurements and expected them to fit me (Shaw, 1907, p. 37).

THE CONCEPTS AND PROCEDURES

Personality and Adjustment

The concepts of personality and adjustment are central to the present investigation of aging. The terms have been used widely by a variety of behavioral scientists and practitioners, and are used in everyday vocabularies. The terms have correspondingly wide meanings. Uses of the concepts have the advantages and disadvantages of breadth of measurement and interpretation; we have tried to avail ourselves of the advantages and to avoid becoming enmeshed in the conceptual and methodological tangles that could be so intellectually inviting.

As we have said, personality is the distinctive pattern of organizing one's perceptions and beliefs and one's way of acting and reacting. This definition is in keeping with Chown's global concept, which includes the individual's attitudes, emotions, motivations, and activity patterns (Chown, 1968, p. 134).

Maddi's definition is interesting as we think about continuity and change:

Personality is a stable set of characteristics and tendencies that determine those commonalities and differences in the psychological behavior (thoughts, feelings, and actions) of people that have continuity in time and that may or may not be easily understood in terms of the social and biological pressures of the immediate situation alone (Maddi, 1968, p. 10).

If one accepted this statement quite literally, there would be no need to investigate change, for this writer's prime concern was obviously with the formed ("congealed") personality in contrast to a forming or re-forming one. However, in his comparative analysis of personality theories, Maddi did offer conclusions pertinent to the question of continuity and change in adult life. He showed that certain models, those he called the "consistency" and "fulfillment" models, do portray personality as changing "fairly continuously" over the life span. "Personality change should occur as a concomitant of the natural process of encountering different events in the world of experience," he said (Maddi, 1968, p. 152).

Maddi's definition reveals the difficulty some might see in conceptualizing personality in relation to its stability and change. Hall and Lindzey's comparative analysis showed that writers differed greatly in the emphasis they gave to development in the first place, and to the continuity or lack of continuity in personality in the second (1970, p. 587).

To us the concepts of personality and adjustment are not easily distinguished except, perhaps, that one describes the characteristic *person* while the other describes the characteristic *process* he uses in his daily activities in meeting his needs and interacting with environmental forces within some social order.

We have tried to see adjustment as a social-psychological process, as one of achieving and of having achieved certain attitudinal conditions and qualities of behavior. Some of these are inferred from such outer manifestations as activity and social participation and interaction, and some are inferred from more personal and private behavior. As such, the concept incorporates both "outer" and "inner" aspects of behavior.

Use of the concept of adjustment generally involves evaluating the degrees to which the person is achieving or has achieved a pattern that encompasses these conditions or qualities. We defined a well-adjusted person as "one who is living a life which is reasonably satisfactory to himself and which meets the expectations of society" (Britton, 1963, p. 61). This means that he is reasonably healthy and that he is a participant in a variety of activities, that he has both personal and specialized contacts with others, and that these interpersonal relations bring him satisfaction. The concept also includes the notion that the individual feels reasonably self-confident and adequate in initiating action and in intellectual functioning. He finds his existence as a human person meaningful and of worth, as one having integrity in his own, if not in some other, scheme of values. He maintains a degree of independence and self-sufficiency and, as viewed by others, he functions appropriately and effectively.

It is assumed that adjustment is dependent upon or influenced by a number of situational and personal factors, and that it will be "good" or "poor" to the degree that these factors pose threats and hinder gratifications of physical, social, and psychological needs. In these ways adjustment is used primarily as a dependent variable. Let us turn to the methods we used in measuring personality and adjustment of older adults.

Criteria and Selection of Procedures

We selected or developed methods for measuring personality and adjustment which presumably could appraise both attitudinal and overt behavior of older persons. The techniques were selected partly on pragmatic bases: they were available and were deemed appropriate and useful for our purposes. Adaptations of existing instruments were made when they appeared to be useful techniques and could fit our purposes. We devised other techniques that were necessary to round out the assessments in accord with our conceptual grounds.

The fact that the research was a *field* project using subjects residing in the open community was important in our thinking about appropriate techniques. Our interest in obtaining a maximally complete study population emphasized this consideration. This meant that problems of establishing and maintaining rapport were critical, especially so when we were asking people to give us their time and attention without direct or obvious benefit to them. Residents' judgments about us as investigators (and for many as "representatives" of the state university) seemed of increasing import especially after the initial liaison period, when we found that our passage to and fro in the study area was so well observed. These matters were all the more crucial when we contemplated making follow-up visits for the longitudinal measurements.

Other thoughts about methodology pertained to our subjects' being "ordinary" community residents. If we were to be successful in getting all, or nearly all, persons to participate in our research, our techniques would have to appeal to and be comprehended by persons of widely varying interests, abilities, and temperaments.

Our techniques had to be readily understood and make sense to the man and woman "on the street" regardless of educational, occupational, or social level. At first this seemed to have special application in this small rural community, but we are convinced that the same point is true in any area where the research subjects are not self-selected on bases of ability or interest.

A major consideration, of course, involved our subjects' age and the characteristics commonly associated with age. At the initial phase of the research all were to be 65 years of age or over, but many would be 75, 80, 90, and even older at that time. In general, this implied certain educational levels, since the number of years of schooling has changed markedly over the years. Probably more important, however, it suggested to us that our subjects would likely take pretty much of a commonsense look at our methods. Whatever technique we used would have to be quite reasonable in the eyes of our subjects. The tasks must be efficiently structured to enable our older subjects to proceed with the greatest ease possible and with the least amount of fatigue, anxiety, and emotional disruption. We could predict that various portions of our interviews or tests would provoke differing emotional responses, but we were to learn quickly that this was a highly varying phenomenon in itself: one interviewee would willingly discuss intimate details of his health but find questions about his family disturbing, while another might reverse this attitude. We wanted our techniques (and our interviewers' procedures) to be seen as interesting and useful, to occasion the least amount of anxiety and emotional irritation, and to be short enough for us to succeed in obtaining our data in a reasonable time. What was "reasonable" to some, however, was not "reasonable" to others!

Another matter relevant to selecting research instruments and defining the task was related to the personnel available for gathering data in the field. While we could train them carefully in field work procedures as *interviewers* for our study of personality and adjustment, we could not expect them to act as clinicians and, for example, to follow any "psychological leads" offered by the subject in the course of a personal interview about himself. This meant that our techniques had to be those which could be administered reliably by competent interviewers who were not trained clinicians.

Selection and Training of Interviewers

In the course of our research, probably every problem we had ever heard about as inherent in longitudinal research, field research, or gerontological research came into our thinking at one point or another. Of these problems, selection of personnel for field work was one of the most crucial. With experience, we grew more confident of our intuitive judgments about how well individuals would relate to our older subjects, how well they could and would follow our procedures and how much they would enhance or weaken the reputation of the study, the investigators, or the university. The interviewers were a varied group: some were graduate or undergraduate male and female students in the social sciences, others were middle-aged women, and one was (and saw herself as) an "older" woman. Most were paid by the hour, while others were paid by salary. They saw themselves challenged in various ways by our directive, which was "to get in, get the interview, and get out, *giving of yourself as it seems appropriate.*" The older woman who helped us as an interviewer in connection with the first-year community-wide survey (see Chapter 2) took as a personal charge the hard-to-get interview, the one in which another interviewer had been put off once or twice or had even been refused. But these challenges were not exclusively hers, for almost all others on our field staffs rose to these tasks with surprising enthusiasm. This seemed particularly true when the authors themselves participated as members of the interviewing teams. Some older residents, having seen the interviewing staff move about the village, even asked to have specific interviewers come their way. One aged man asked for the most attractive young woman interviewer to talk with him; in one of the follow-up sessions another said he would simply wait until Mrs. T. returned because he wanted to visit with her again.

These anecdotes exemplify the varying stances that individuals take in connection with field research, and illustrate some of the effects of personnel in the field. We were sensitive to the community being rural and to the fact that its members were fairly conservative—for example, in their views about dress or personal style of behavior. We tried to blend and to help our interviewers to blend appropriately into the setting. This we did partly because we wanted to obtain behavioral data that were characteristic of the community and its residents in their *natural* states insofar as this was possible. Indeed this was our basic objective. In addition, however, we felt that we should blend because of the basic *respect* we held for our subjects as *persons* and for the locale as a *community* to which they were devoted. Their comments about the area being a very pleasant one in which to live and work (and grow old) often stressed this attachment, and we tried to show genuine appreciation of these views. We were also mindful that such behavior was necessary if our research objectives were to be met.

Our interviewers were provided housing in a neighboring community partly because accommodations were available there and partly to enable staff discussions to be held without danger of being overheard or misunderstood. In addition, the interviewers needed the opportunity to relax and to complete their reports with freedom from observation by the subjects or potential subjects.

As we have said, one instruction to our interviewers was to "give something of yourselves" to the interviewees. In a sense this was simply a directive to be friendly, affable, and courteous, but it was more: we wanted our staff to provide a breath of fresh thought or conversation, perhaps about themselves or their activities, a bit of social diversion that would interest the residents with whom they were talking. This would come naturally, we thought, to the kind of people we had engaged as interviewers, but we emphasized to them our sense of the value of this element as a means of maintaining rapport and also as a way of respectful but minimal repayment for the time and effort the subjects had given. No subject was paid in money for participating, and we believe they would have felt we were squandering (public) funds if we had offered such payment; they could not have been bought!

It is possible that the interviewer behavior we rather unsystematically introduced may have had some effect on our results. We honestly believe that our interviewing techniques did not cause the interviewees to bias their response in one direction or another. We also believe that we obtained *good* cooperation within the community for a variety of reasons, including the respect and warmth we encouraged our interviewers to express to all whom they met.

All the field work procedures were pretested and evaluated with pilot subjects in settings similar to those of the investigation. By the use of "dry-run" interviews, field workers gained experience in the interviewing and testing techniques of the study. During each of the four periods of intensive field work, one person was named as supervisor and was responsible for the general direction of the project, under the overall leadership and administration of the investigators.

THE MEASURES AND THEIR USE

The data being gathered directly from older subjects were obtained through the use of an interview-testing session. (The schedule used in the initial interview is given in Appendix D; the schedule used in the subsequent years was revised slightly to incorporate information about change since the first assessment.) The total procedure was expected to take little more than an hour per subject, although generally it turned out to take more, largely because our older interviewees often liked having an opportunity to talk. (The maximum time spent was close to three hours, but usually the interview took one and a half to two hours.) The measures administered during the session with the subject included all those derived from the subject directly: Chicago Activity Inventory, Chicago Attitude Inventory, Personal Relations and Sociability Scale, Opinion Conformity Scale, and Thematic Apperception Test. Two other measures used the interview data and impressions made during the interview: the Judge's Rating and the Interviewer's Rating. Each of these measures will be described, and information available on its reliability and validity will be presented. The techniques of administering the instrument and of scoring or evaluating the data will be recounted.

Two additional techniques grew out of our interest in seeing old people in their natural family and community environment. Data for one came from the community-wide survey in 1955, when we sought a Reputation Rating for our subjects. This involved almost, by definition, selected individuals. Another measure was used with a sample of selected subjects who were evaluated by a panel of members of the community: the Community Rating. The nature of these two measures will be sketched briefly in this section; in Chapter 5 we shall explain these measures more fully in the course of a discussion of our older adults as members of the community.

Chicago Activity Inventory

This measure concerns a subject's reports of his participation in the everyday activities of living. Devised by Burgess, Cavan, and Havighurst (Cavan, Burgess, Havighurst, and Goldhamer, 1949) at the University of Chicago, the technique was developed following efforts of the Social Science Research Council to provide tools for study of the problems of old people (Pollak, 1948). The Activity Inventory assumes that the well-adjusted person is reasonably healthy and engages in a number of varied activities. Objective questions concerning actual participation and health problems are used to obtain answers that are grouped and scored in five sections. Each item has its own weighted scoring scheme.

One group of six items made up the so-called intimate contacts activity score, including the questions about (1) with whom the subject is living, (2) how often he sees his family, (3) the extent to which he feels his family neglects him and/or (4) interferes in his affairs, (5) the number of close friends he says he has, and (6) the frequency with which he visits with his children. On the first item, for instance, the subject is scored with 2 when he lives with his spouse or with his spouse and children; he is scored with 0 when he lives with anyone else.

Additional subscores of the Activity Inventory were obtained on leisure activities, religious activities, health, and economic security. Cavan et al. (1949) assumed that the last two areas were highly correlated with actual engagement in personal and social activities, and they included such items as a rating of one's present health and economic position.

Each subsection had a possible score of 12; the total possible score on the Activity Inventory was 60. Scoring was completed by staff personnel under the supervision of the investigators.

The questions on the Activity Inventory were arranged within the interview in places where they would be logical in their sequence; they were interspersed with items from the other measures. The interviewers followed the precise wording of the questions insofar as possible, and departed from it only when it was necessary to make the meaning clear.

Thus the Chicago Activity Inventory uses the subject's statements about his overt activities and his health and economic security. Data on reliability provided by Cavan et al. showed test-retest agreement from 62 to 82 percent for the complete scale. Using a split-halves method, a reliability coefficient of .66 was obtained, but Cavan et al. considered this figure an underestimation because of the difficulties in pairing items.

Validity coefficients were obtained by correlating Activity Inventory scores with external "checklists" and "word portraits." The correlation of the Activity Inventory with a combined score of these two measures was .65. Correlated with the Attitude Inventory, the coefficient was .78 (Cavan et al., 1949, pp. 137-142).

Chicago Attitude Inventory

The Chicago Attitude Inventory (Cavan et al., 1949) is based on the assumption that the well-adjusted person finds *satisfaction* in the ordinary affairs and activities of life and that he enjoys general feelings of happiness and usefulness.

Eight sections of items are included: health, friends, work, economic security, religion, usefulness, happiness, and family relationships. Each section has seven items. The interviewee was asked to agree or disagree with each item—for example, "I have more friends now than ever before" and "I am happy only when I have definite work to do."

We arranged the items in a "cyclical" format, one item from one section followed by one item from another section, with items from the Personal Relations (P) and Sociability (S) Scales inserted periodically. The seven items from each section of the Attitude Inventory were scored according to a standardized system, three items in each section being scored positively and three items negatively; a seventh item was a neutral item and was not scored. The item scores are added algebraically and a constant of 3 is added to clear negative numbers. Thus the total possible score per section was 6; the total for the Attitude Inventory, 48.

The reliability of the total Attitude Inventory is shown by a test-retest correlation of .72; the interval between testings varied from two weeks to two months. With a split-halves method, the product-moment correlation was .90; it increased to .95 by application of the Spearman-Brown formula (Cavan et al., 1949, pp. 121-136). Again using "word portraits," "check-lists," and a combination of the two, correlation coefficients with the Attitude Inventory were, respectively, .49, .50, and .53 (Cavan et al., 1949, pp. 121-136; Havighurst, 1951).

Personal Relations and Sociability Scales

When Guilford and Zimmerman (1949) constructed their Temperament Survey, they set out to provide a paper-pencil personality survey of ten unique personality traits which had been identified by factor analysis. The utility of the traits had been demonstrated by clinical and counseling applications. The traits included, for example, general activity, ascendance, and objectivity. Ten scales were developed, each containing 30 items, each to be answered on a yes-no (agree-disagree) basis.

Guilford and Zimmerman included attitudes toward relations with other persons. Their Personal Relations (P) Scale "has consistently correlated highest with all criteria involving human relations. It seems to represent the core of 'getting along with others'. . . . A high score means tolerance and understanding of other people and their human weaknesses. A low score indicates fault-finding and criticalness of other people and of institutions generally. The low-scoring person is not likely to 'get along with others' " (Guilford and Zimmerman, 1949, p. 9).

As Guilford and Zimmerman prepared the P Scale, it contained 30 items, including, for example:

154. You would change a lot of things about human nature if you could have your way about it. (The "correct" answer is "no.")
199. Most people today try to do an honest day's work for a day's pay. (The "correct" answer is "yes.")
254. Some people pay more attention to your comings and goings than they should. (The "correct" answer is "no.")

The reliability coefficient for the P Scale was reported as .80, based upon the Kuder-Richardson formula applied to men and women combined. Their normative population was college students.

Thirteen items were selected from the P Scale and adapted for use in our format with our subjects. Selection was based upon judged relevance to older persons. The items above were made to read, respectively, as follows:

154. If you could have your way, would you change a lot of things about human nature?
199. Do you agree with this?—Most people try to do an honest day's work for a day's pay.
254. Do you think some people pay too much attention to your business?

Guilford and Zimmerman's Sociability (S) Scale was described as useful "wherever the trait of social participation is a consideration. The high and low scores indicate the contrast between the person who is at ease with others, enjoys their company and readily establishes intimate rapport, versus the withdrawn, reserved person who is hard to get to know" (1949, p. 9). This scale originally contained 30 items and had a reliability coefficient of .87. Ten items were selected and adapted for our use. For instance, the item (No. 29) "You enjoy getting acquainted with people" became "Do you enjoy getting to know people?" (The "correct" answer is "yes.") The item (No. 69) "After being introduced to someone, you just cannot think of things to say to make good conversation" was revised: "When you meet someone new do you have a hard time thinking of things to say?" (The "correct" answer is "no.")

The 13 P Scale items and the 10 from the S Scale were inserted in a prescribed "cyclical" order within the Attitude Inventory. The items were scored according to the original Temperament Survey directions and the two scores were combined by simple addition. These scales were included because we felt that the interpersonal dimensions of our personality-adjustment syndrome needed to be additionally represented in our measurement procedures.

Opinion Conformity Scale

This procedure was constructed specifically for the present research. It was based upon the reasoning that a degree of conformity of behavior is necessary if an individual is to be well-adjusted, especially in a small community. From the opinions gathered in our 1955 house-to-house survey of the study area, we derived what we felt was the consensus of community views about older people (Lansing, 1956). These were in four areas: family relationships (Britton, Mather, and Lansing, 1961a), work and retirement (Britton, Mather, and Lansing, 1961b), community participation (Britton, Mather, and Lansing, 1962), and the solving of personal problems (Britton and Britton, 1962). These findings are summarized in the present report (Chapter 5), and some conclusions are drawn from them about the nature of our small community as a place in which to live and grow old.

On the basis of normative data in these four areas of behavior, we devised twelve items in order to determine the extent of our older subjects' yes-no agreement with the predominant opinions of the community. For example, the subject was asked these questions:

1. Should the family of an older couple help if the couple is almost out of money?
2. Should a person hold on to a job just as long as he is physically able?

The twelve items making up the Opinion Conformity Scale (shown by asterisks on the interview schedule in Appendix D) were scored according to whether or not the answers agreed with the consensus views of the community as defined by our procedures. The score was the number of such "correct" responses, the total possible being 12.

Thematic Apperception Test

The Thematic Apperception Test (TAT) is a well-known projective test of personality and adjustment (Murray, 1943). With this method the subject "is shown pictures susceptible to many different interpretations and is invited to make up stories about them. The ambiguous character of the material precludes merely conventional answers and forces the subject to fall back on his own preferred ways of doing things. He is thus apt to reveal certain covert features of his personality, for example his unsatisfied desires, suppressed anxieties, preferred patterns for perceiving the world and the people around him" (White, 1966, p. 100).

We selected three cards from Murray's original set to use as a means through which the subject could "project" the less conscious or unconscious aspects of his personality and adjustment pattern. The three cards were selected on the basis of their possible saliency for older persons and for the possibility that older adults generally could identify with a presumed older figure in each picture. The pictures selected were 7 BM, 6 BM, and 10, usually (but not always) seen as follows: an older and younger man talking together (7 BM); an older woman and a younger man, often seen as her son (6 BM); and a close-up view of an older man and woman, often seen as in an embrace (10).

The usual procedure calls for the subject simply to tell a story about the picture. As generally used in assessment procedures, the essentials of a story include the identity of those in the picture, what is happening, what each person in the story is thinking and feeling, and what the outcome will be. We tried out the usual TAT procedure in pilot interview situations and found that older persons resisted and were frustrated by the method and that they required much encouragement to respond at all. Their responses were typically very brief and meager, and often they did not include the essentials for a psychological appraisal to be made.

We felt it necessary, therefore, to modify the usual procedure in order to obtain the necessary data. We devised a "standardized probing scheme" which we felt our nonclinician interviewers could use effectively with our subjects. The directions to the subjects were as follows:

> Now this is where we want you to use your imagination. I have some pictures here *(hold up cards without revealing the picture sides)* and I'm going to show them to you one at a time.
>
> I'd like you to look at the picture, think about it for a moment, and then say what you think is going on in the picture. Just make up a story about it. Whatever you say will be all right. You can make up any kind of story you want to. Don't forget to use your imagination.
>
> Here's the first picture. *(Expose card No. 7 BM and hand it to S. Wait for a response, record it, and continue to wait and record until the story has been completed or until you judge that S needs prodding to finish the task.)*

After the initial response the interviewer's job was to determine which of the essential elements of the respondent's story was not yet provided and then (in the case of the first picture) to ask one or another of the following probing questions:

What are the people doing in that picture? What's happening?
What is the older man thinking about?
What is the younger man thinking about?
How does the older man feel?
How does the younger man feel?
What happened before this?
How will it all turn out in the end?

Three pictures from the TAT were used to provide sufficient opportunity for the subject to reveal himself in this projective manner while not overtaxing him or jeopardizing the collection of other data.

We assumed that our subjects were identifying with the older person in the picture, independent of sex, and our analysis of the stories was built upon this assumption. The subject's characterization of the main older person in each story was evaluated on seven-point rating scales in terms of his adequacy in initiating action, his self-confidence, intellectual functioning, happiness, social status, and interpersonal acceptance. Fifty such scales were devised and, after trial use with "dry-run" interviews, were used by judges who rated the TAT material independently of other data about the subject; 34 of the scales were used in the final scoring procedure. (In addition, the judges assessed the story as a whole according to how many ideas the subject presented, how definite these ideas were, how happy the outcome of the story was, or how appropriate and organized the story seemed to be. This information has not been used in the present work.) The rating sheet and outline for the TAT analysis are included in Appendix E.

The story for each picture was rated separately and independently; the total possible score for each TAT card was 238 (that is, $34 \times 7 = 238$); for the three cards, 714. For a subject's TAT material to be used, scorable responses must have been made on at least two of the three cards; if he responded to only two of the pictures, a mean of those two scores was assigned to the third.

For the 1956 material three trained judges rated the stories. Interjudge agreement on total scores for 23 subjects was shown by correlations of .88, .93, and .98. The 1962 data were rated by two judges, and the interjudge correlation on total scores for 21 subjects was .86. For the 1965 material two judges again rated the stories, and the interjudge correlation for 38 subjects (29 of them being longitudinal subjects) was .99. Different judges were used for the responses for the three years.[1]

Judge's Rating

This assessment of adjustment, devised by Ruth Shonle Cavan as the Cavan Adjustment Rating Scale, was used by Havighurst and Albrecht (1953) in their research with older people in a midwest community. It consists of six rating scales followed by a master rating. Three scales have to do with primary and secondary relations and with activities outside of groups; three other scales represent certain attitudes that are central to personal adjustment. The master scale is a "flexible summary" of the six more specific scales, a rating of the "general degree of personal adjustment." In using this scale the rater takes account of all the information available from the interview and "he weighs the separate scales in accordance with what seems to him their importance in the individual case" (Havighurst and Albrecht, 1953, p. 407).

The idea is to obtain general overall judgments about the subject—"to put meaning into the interview by making inferences and interpretations of the interview data," as we instructed the judges. We asked them to interpret the material quite liberally, i.e., to use their own judgments and impressions of the subject. We did not use the interviewer's reports or ratings for these evaluations.

The scales of the Judge's Rating, as we have called the measure, were ten-point scales with descriptive words or phrases along the scale. The subscales were as follows: (1) primary or personal, intimate contacts (to illustrate, points on the scale ranged from being "alone in the world, no family, relatives, friends" at the 0-1 end to having "daily contacts, group probably of long standing, closely incorporated into group life, important in determining group actions" at the 8-9 end); (2) secondary or more formal and specialized contacts; (3) activities outside groups; (4) attitude of emotional security in small group or in religion; (5)

---

[1] The interjudge correlations should be viewed with caution. Because of the dearth of response material, both raters necessarily placed many ratings in the middle category of the rating scale, indicating that neither end-point adjective applied. Thus, the extent of agreement appears higher than it actually was.

status or feeling of importance; (6) happiness and contentment; and (7) master rating on personal adjustment (Appendix F).

In the Havighurst-Albrecht investigation, the *master* rating correlated .73 with the Chicago Attitude Inventory (1953, p. 286).

In our use of these scales we omitted the third scale, activities outside groups, since our early raters found that our interview typically solicited little or no information in this area. Six scales were used; the possible score, then, was 9 × 6 = 54.

The reliability of ratings is shown by interjudge agreement correlations. Three judges rated the 1956 material for 25 subjects, with interjudge correlations of .82, .82, and .88, indicating substantial but not complete agreement among them. Two judges made the judgments for 1962 data; for 19 subjects the inter-rater correlation was .86. The correlations of three judges' ratings of the 1965 material were .53, .62, and .59; because of these low intercorrelations we used "consensus" ratings, where raters pooled their thoughts and agreed on a rating. The agreement of the judges with the consensus ratings for 46 subjects is shown by correlations of .80, .83, and .85.

Interviewer's Rating

Early in the research we wished to have a record of the interviewer's observations of the interviewee as a person and of the extent to which investigators could communicate and interact with him. We devised six simple scales, each with five points, with the end-points labeled as follows: (1) *vision* —poor versus good; (2) *hearing*—poor versus good; (3) *attention and concentration* —mind wandered frequently versus attentive during entire interview; (4) *interaction with interviewer*—no contact versus very responsive; (5) *interest*—very casual interest versus intense interest; and (6) *cooperativeness*—barely civil versus went out of his way to be helpful. In addition, the interviewer was asked to write evaluative comments about the interview situation and information pertinent to the interviewee's personal adjustment not otherwise covered (Appendix G).

As the longitudinal aspects of the research proceeded, we decided that these six scales provided important behavioral data based upon direct observation, albeit subjectively seen and rated.

They supplied a useful addition, we thought, to the data provided by our other techniques. We entered them, then, into our analyses. In addition, the ratings and the comments helped to guide us in planning our follow-up contacts with the subjects.

The total possible score on the Interviewer's Rating was $6 \times 5 = 30$.

We might comment, somewhat parenthetically, that over the years of the study we became increasingly sensitive to the attrition in our subject population and to our subjects' growing older and becoming less able to participate in our rather lengthy asessment procedures. Simultaneously we became less captivated by self-reports and more interested in information and evaluations obtained by observation. This was true partly because of our views of the inherent nature of the data and partly because we became more confident of ourselves and our staff members as observers. It was also true because we felt that, as our subjects advanced in age, we needed techniques that could provide us with additional useful information at little or no cost in their time or effort. Our techniques simply were a strain for too many of them.

In 1962 we asked our interviewers to add the use of the Life Satisfaction Scales, which had recently become available (Neugarten, Havighurst, and Tobin, 1961); in 1965 we expanded the observers' evaluations still further to provide some information on such things as the subject's mental ability, his capacity for independent living, and his engagement in social aspects of living, especially those outside the home. In addition, we asked for more description of the environment, including the subject's socioeconomic status and the general condition of his residence.

Since our emphasis in this report is on change and continuity, we have given more prominence to the longitudinal information on the subjects than to data available only at selected points in the time span of the study.

Community Rating

Early in our thinking about the research we became interested in working out ways of checking how well our psychometric methods using self-reports of our subjects corresponded to the evaluations of them by a peer group. The Community Rating was devised for this purpose for use with a sample of the study population (Britton, 1959). Necessary to the procedure were older persons so well known in the community that they could be evaluated *and* also members of the community who knew older individuals sufficiently well to be able to assess them on the dimensions of interest in our project. Thus we had to locate community members who (we said arbitrarily) were not themselves eligible by age as subjects, who knew a maximum number of subjects, and who could be reasonably objective and reliable in making an evaluation. We also had to identify those of our older subjects who were sufficiently well known to be evaluated. The interview we used with the selected individuals appears as Appendix H.

Our procedure had to be one which would discriminate among our subjects. We worked out a "Q-sort" (Stevenson, 1953) procedure that forced the raters to make discriminations on five dimensions relevant to social-psychological functioning within a community: respect, value of opinion, conformity, considerateness, and number of friends. In 1956 we used this procedure first with some 17 panelists concerning 25 selected subjects; in 1962 and 1965, certain of the panelists used the procedure again with surviving subjects. We called the subjects the Q group; the raters were denoted as Q panelists.

This procedure is described more completely in Chapter 5, along with details of the findings. They are presented when we consider the small rural community as a place to live and grow old.

Reputation Rating

Another technique was also possible within our small study community, considering the presumedly relative intimacy of its social relationships—the Reputation Rating. In the course of our community-wide survey of 1955 (Appendix C), we sought the names of individuals who were managing well or not so well in certain behavioral areas in their old age. These data indicated the reputations of some of our older subjects within the local milieu; naturally not all our subjects were equally visible or equally likely to be mentioned, and hence this type of information is on selected persons. We use these data primarily in connection with our discussion of the community in Chapter 5, where we shall examine the procedure more thoroughly.

WAIS Similarities Scale

In 1965 a measure of intellectual functioning was added to the longitudinal test battery, primarily for the purpose of providing information relevant to survival. The Similarities Scale from Wechsler's 1955 version of his Adult Intelligence Scale (WAIS) was selected for the purpose of estimating intellectual behavior in a standardized form. Wechsler indicated that the Similarities Scale was relatively easy to give and had interest appeal for the average adult. In addition, this scale was recognized as containing a great amount of a "general intellectual factor" as contrasted with more specific intellectual abilities.

Our success with its use was mixed. While it seemed to follow our other procedures quite naturally, many of our subjects viewed it with skepticism. Almost facetiously they replied to the initial question of how an orange and a banana are alike with a comment such as "Well, I don't know about that, but they sure are expensive these days!" Or, to the question of how north and west are alike, some responded as to how cold the winds were when they came from the north in comparison to the west.

Nevertheless, at our third round of testing, we used the WAIS Similarities Scale. The protocols were scored independently by two psychologists, with an inter-scorer reliability coefficient of .98; where they differed, a mean score was used. The standard scoring criteria were used, and raw scores and age-scaled scores were derived (Wechsler, 1955).

Data derived from the WAIS are used in the case study presentations later in this chapter and in connection with the analyses of factors related to survival in Chapter 4.

THE METHODS OF ANALYSIS

Data Processing

The sources of data in the present research include community members "at large," especially selected panelists, older persons themselves, observer-interviewers, and "experts" who evaluated material collected by others. Interviews, tests, and observations provided the basic data, which were transformed to quantitative scores or ratings. These quantitative data have been processed by standard procedures of analysis to provide descriptive information about our subjects as groups: frequency distributions, means, medians, ranges, standard and average deviations.

Longitudinal Trend Score

A main interest of ours was, of course, in *individual* continuity or change over time and with factors related to it. For this analysis we devised a Longitudinal Trend Score (LTS). To show *individual change* we wanted a method that would show the *direction* of change and the *degree* of change, if any, over the time of the research. A correlation coefficient provides an indicator of direction and of degree, and if *time* were included as one variable and each measure in turn as the other variable in a correlation, we could then have an index of change with time for each of the personality-adjustment measures. This method provided a simple statistical means of analyzing individual change over time.

The Longitudinal Trend Score was actually the product-moment correlation between the years or times of assessment (1956-1962-1965 as one variable) and the individual's scores on a measure for those years (as the other variable). Thus an LTS of +.90, for example, for the Activity Inventory, would mean a high, positive correlation between the years of assessment, on the one hand, and the same individual's scores on the Activity Inventory for those respective years. This individual's LTS of +.90 for Activity Inventory, then, shows a marked positive change over the years, compared, say, with a person whose LTS was +.30. One whose LTS was zero would not have changed, and one whose LTS was −.90 would have declined on the measure over the years of the study. For an LTS to be calculated, measures for all three years must have been available, and this fact accounts for the variability in N's among our LTS's.

The Longitudinal Trend Scores are presented later in frequency distributions with indicators of range and central tendency. We grouped them according to those of +.50 and above, indicating that these showed marked positive change; −.49 to +.49, which showed little or no change one way or another; and −.50 and higher, which showed marked negative change over the years.

To show how changes in our measures of personality and adjustment were associated with various personal and social factors, we compared subjects according to their LTS's by means of Fisher's Exact Probability Test or chi-square. In addition, to show the dynamics of individual change or stability, we chose subjects for portrayal here also according to their LTS's, listed for each subject on each of the several measures. These lists assisted us in selecting subjects whom we could describe as "maintaining," "declining," or "improving" themselves on our measures. We classified some individuals predominately in these categories insofar as possible, and selected several to describe here as individual case studies. In this method our interest was in putting all available data together and drawing some generalizations from them.

CONTINUITY AND CHANGE—THE FINDINGS

Objective

A major objective of the present study was to observe continuity and change in older adults who were living in an ordinary, open community setting. To reach this objective required that we collect data concerning the same individuals over a considerable period of time. More or less complete interview material, including measurements of personality and adjustment, must have been available on each individual at the three points of assessment if he was to be included. Seventeen men and 29 women were qualified, and we refer to them as the "longitudinal study population."

In this section we shall (1) describe the longitudinal study group in terms of background information gained through the three interviews, (2) describe the group in terms of their performance on the measures of personality and adjustment, (3) present, by means of Longitudinal Trend Scores, an analysis of how the group changed or remained stable over the nine-year period of the study, and (4) attempt to isolate factors related to change or stability in the group of subjects and in individuals, some of whose lives we shall examine more closely.

Description of the Longitudinal Subjects

The longitudinal subjects were interviewed and tested at all three assessment periods in the study: 1956, 1962, and 1965. They represent a "fixed sample," assessed by repeated measurements. As we show in Chapter 4, they were obviously persons who survived the years of the study and were also able, willing, and available to be interviewed and tested. Thus, some persons were removed from the study by death, others by moving from the area, others by refusing to participate in the research, while still others eliminated themselves or were eliminated by family members or friends because they were "too old" or "too ill" to participate. In all instances, such information was verified. Friendly attempts were made—considerably short of coercion, however—by the staff to encourage participation in the study, but some felt that the procedures were too taxing emotionally or not of sufficient worth to participate again. We believe that some sincerely wanted to "help out" the investigators but felt it necessary to protect themselves from the "stirrings" that our questions sometimes aroused. Others said they were atypical and that their histories or attitudes could be of no conceivable value to others. For some our repeated contact was reason enough to refuse: "I did that once and I don't want to do it again." While we know of no apparent and deliberate attempt on the part of any person in the community to arouse distrust of the investigators or the study, it was clear that our comings and goings within the community were a matter of comment among the older residents. Some regarded the experience of our interview as an opportunity for self-assessment, apparently, and sometimes they expressed pleasure for a chance to talk about themselves.

At the three points of data collection—1956, 1962, and 1965—the longitudinal subjects who were interviewed and tested constituted 83 percent, 85 percent, and 76 percent, respectively, of those who were eligible as subjects (Chapter 4). These persons clearly represent a select group from the point of view of survival, but we are convinced that they are at the same time the maximum number available under the circumstances and that they are reasonably representative of those eligible to be assessed.

Descriptive information on the longitudinal subjects is presented in Tables 2 to 8. Such information was obtained by direct interview with individual subjects and was verified, in the case of age, by cross-checking with information obtained in the original community-wide survey. (Only one person, a woman, refused to give her age.)

Age and Era

As shown in Table 2, the ages of the longitudinal subjects at the first assessment point ranged from 65 to 85 for the men and 65 to 80 for the women; about one-half of all were between 65 and 69 years of age. At the third point, in 1965, the ages ranged from 74 to 94 for the men and 73 to 89 for the women, when nearly three-fourths were between 75 and 84 years of age. On the average, both men and women at the three points were approximately 71, 77, and 80 years of age, but the women varied somewhat less from the average than did the men (as shown by their smaller standard deviations and ranges).

TABLE 2

Age of Longitudinal Ss, by Percent[a]

	Men (N = 17)			Women (N = 29)		
Item	*1956*	*1962*	*1965*	*1956*	*1962*	*1965*
Age						
90-94 years	—	12	12	—	—	—
85-89 years	12	6	6	—	4	14
80-84 years	—	12	18	3	35	41
75-79 years	18	29	53	14	17	31
70-74 years	18	41	12	38	45	14
65-69 years	53	—	—	45	—	—
Range	65-85	71-91	74-94	65-80	70-86	73-89
Mean	71.35	77.35	80.35	70.69	76.69	79.69
Standard deviation	6.48	6.48	6.48	4.59	4.59	4.59

[a]Percentages in tables may not total 100 due to rounding.

Our subjects, then, were individuals born in the twenty-year post-Civil War period from 1871 to 1891. Most of them would have been children during the late Victorian era, in their twenties or thirties at the time of World War I, in their forties or fifties at the time of the Great Depression, and in their fifties or sixties at the onset of World War II. They were in school just before and/or just after the turn of the century, during the McKinley-Theodore Roosevelt administrations. They were homemakers or young farmers or at work in other occupations or serving in the armed forces during World War I. In middle age, many of them knew intimately the effects of economic hardship during the 1930's and the distress of war again for their children and grandchildren in the 1940's.

Most of the subjects undoubtedly expected their own farms and savings, meager in a number of instances, to support their needs in old age. They scarcely expected to receive governmental pension benefits themselves, since before 1956 self-employed farmers, as one group, were not eligible to receive Social Security. (They may well have been initially opposed to such "handout" programs.) Neither did they expect their buying power to diminish as it did during the inflationary years of the 1950's and 1960's!

Educational Attainment

Table 3 presents information concerning the education and occupation of the longitudinal subjects. Small percentages of persons (one man and two women) had not completed eight grades of school. One-third of the men and nearly half of the women, then, had not attended high school. (This might be compared to the nearly three-quarters of individuals 65 and over in 1966 in the United States as a whole who had not attended high school [Brotman, 1967, census data].) On the other hand, about two-thirds of the men and half of the women in the study had completed high school or had had some college.

In spite of their being from a rural environment, our subjects are as a group somewhat better educated than older persons generally in the United States. The fact that our subjects were virtually all native to the study area, plus the fact that there was an "academy" in Pennsboro at the time our subjects would have been eligible for such an educational opportunity, may account for their somewhat higher educational level.

Occupational Status

In 1956 the interviewees were asked, "What work have you done most of the time during your adult years?" In the case of a housewife or a widow who had never been in the labor force, the question pertained to the husband. The replies, which provide some indication of social status, were grouped into three categories (Table 3). Not quite two-thirds of the longitudinal subjects

TABLE 3

Education and Occupation of Longitudinal
Ss (1956), by Percent

Item	Men	Women
Education (N)	(16)	(29)
College completed or beyond	13	3
Some college	13	21
High school completed	38	24
Some high school	—	7
Eight grades completed	31	38
Less than 8 grades	6	7
Occupation or former occupation of family wage earner (N)	(17)	(29)
Occupation Group A: Professional, technical workers; managers, officials, proprietors, except farm	59	55
Occupation Group B: Farmers, farm managers; clerical, sales, kindred workers; craftsmen, foremen, operatives	41	41
Occupation Group C: Farm laborers and foremen; domestic service workers; laborers, except farm	—	4

(59 percent of the men and 55 percent of the women) were
classified as belonging to Occupational Group A, which comprised
professional, technical workers, managers, officials, and propri-
etors. About 40 percent of both men and women were in
Occupational Group B, consisting of farmers, farm managers,
clerical, sales and kindred workers, craftsmen, foremen, and
operatives. Since the community has little industry, few industrial
workers were represented, and there were few professional
persons. Generally, the longitudinal subjects came from middle-
class families, perhaps "lower-middle" and "middle-middle" class.

Health

In the interviews at each assessment period, subjects were
asked questions concerning their health (Table 4). These questions

TABLE 4

Health Information on Longitudinal Ss, by Percent

	Men			Women		
Item	1956	1962	1965	1956	1962	1965
Self-rating on health (N)	(16)	(16)	(17)	(27)	(27)	(29)
Excellent	6	—	—	11	15	7
Good	38	63	41	52	59	52
Fair	44	38	53	26	26	34
Poor or very poor	13	—	6	11	—	6
Number of serious physical problems (N)	(17)	(15)	(16)	(28)	(27)	(29)
Five or more	—	7	6	7	7	7
Three or four	29	47	31	29	44	38
One or two	59	40	56	54	37	41
None	12	7	6	11	11	14
Number of physical difficulties (N)	(17)	(16)	(16)	(28)	(26)	(27)
Five or more	18	25	13	29	31	30
Three or four	41	31	25	32	35	26
One or two	41	31	56	21	23	22
None	—	13	6	18	12	22
Number of psychosomatic ailments (N)	(17)	(15)	(15)	(28)	(27)	(28)
Five or more	12	7	7	32	11	21
Three or four	12	13	27	36	33	39
One or two	65	67	53	18	44	29
None	12	13	13	14	11	11

included a self-rating on health status, a checklist of serious physical problems and physical difficulties, and a checklist of psychosomatic ailments. In general, women seemed to rate their health somewhat better than did men; fewer women rated their health as fair or poor, and more women reported their health to be excellent at all three points in time. All subjects avoided the extremes and often used as a reference point, "for a person my age." Of course these persons were the survivors of a considerably larger cohort group, and they may have been thinking about their health in relation to their own previous health or in relation to others in their age group who were not faring as well as they or who indeed were no longer living.

The interviewer read a list of serious physical problems, including, for example, poor sight, deafness, rheumatic stiffness, heart or stomach trouble, or high blood pressure. The interviewee was to indicate which of these were his. At the three points of contact few of the subjects said they were free of these problems, and most had one or two of them. Men and women did not differ greatly in the number of reported problems, and as groups they changed rather little in the numbers of these problems they checked over the years. These men and women frequently reported their recent contacts with physicians, usually with one or the other of two general practitioners who served the community.

Other physical difficulties, such as shortness of breath, heartburn, feeling tired, difficulty in urination, and headaches, were included in a list of 13 items read to each subject by the interviewer. The number of such difficulties reported is shown in Table 4. More women than men replied that they had *none* of those mentioned, but women tended to have more difficulties than men when they did have some. As a group, the women reported about the same number of difficulties over the years.

A third checklist concerned a number of complaints thought of sometimes as psychosomatic ailments or neurotic symptoms. The list included sleeplessness, bad dreams, "feeling blue," and nervousness. About one-eighth of the longitudinal group, both men and women, indicated they were troubled by none of the items mentioned in the interview. Women apparently were bothered by more of these ailments more often than men at all three periods of time, with between one-half and two-thirds of the men mentioning being troubled by one one or two of those listed. Considerably fewer women had only one or two of these problems; fairly large percentages of them had three, four, or five or more of such ailments. It may have been that the men felt they should not admit having the types of troubles listed, recognizing them as signs of hypersensitivity or malcontent, but it may be that these men had had more exposure to minor irritations and had found it possible to take such irritations in their stride.

In summary, in terms of health, the men of the longitudinal group rated their health less favorably than the women rated theirs, and the group as a whole tended to remain rather stable in their reports of health over the years. Although no trend toward decline or improvement is apparent *in the group*, individuals may have experienced important changes in health over the years.

Family Relationships

Table 5 provides information concerning the marital status and numbers of children of the longitudinal subjects, plus the frequency of their seeing families. Answers to questions about their feelings of neglect and about interference by family are also

TABLE 5

Family Information on Longitudinal Ss, by Percent

Item	Men			Women		
	1956	*1962*	*1965*	*1956*	*1962*	*1965*
Marital status (N)	(17)	(17)	(17)	(29)	(29)	(29)
Married, living with spouse	77	53	53	38	31	31
Separated or divorced	6	6	6	4	—	—
Widowed	18	41	41	35	45	45
Never married	—	—	—	24	24	24
Living arrangements (N)	(17)	(17)	(17)	(29)	(29)	(29)
With husband or wife	47	29	35	35	21	21
With H/W and children	29	24	18	4	14	14
With children alone	6	18	18	18	31	31
Alone	12	24	24	28	24	24
With others	6	6	6	17	10	10
Number of living children (N)	(17)	(16)	(14)	(28)	(27)	(27)
Four or more	41	44	43	39	44	37
Two or three	35	38	43	29	26	26
One	12	6	7	7	7	11
None	12	13	7	25	22	26
Frequency of seeing family (N)	(17)	(16)	(15)	(27)	(25)	(28)
Every day	59	75	27	70	64	32
Once or twice a week	29	13	33	11	16	39
Once a month or less	12	13	40	19	20	29
Feelings about family neglect (N)	(17)	(16)	(14)	(26)	(25)	(28)
Yes, completely	—	—	7	—	—	4
Yes, a little	—	—	—	—	—	11
Not at all	100	100	93	100	100	86
Feelings about family interference (N)	(17)	(16)	(13)	(26)	(25)	(28)
Yes, often	—	—	8	—	—	—
Yes, once in a while	18	—	—	8	—	4
Almost never	82	100	92	92	100	96

reported. More of the men were married and living with their spouses than were women—e.g., in 1956, 77 percent compared with 38 percent. There was a disproportionate number of women who were unmarried and living alone and, consequently, a disproportionate number of women who had no children. (For the total group, the mean number of living children was 4.5, indicating that among the study group fairly large families were common.) More women than men were living with their children, and more women tended to live with others, usually siblings, than did men. Over the time period of the study the group as a whole remained fairly stable as far as marital status and living arrangements were concerned, except that there was an increase in those widowed and a decrease in those married and living with spouses.

At the first two points of the study, a majority of the subjects saw members of the family every day, but over the years both men and women reported seeing their families less frequently. This was apparently true in spite of the subjects' increased age and, presumably and concomitantly, a greater need to see and to be seen by their families. However, it must also be noted that the older subjects reported no marked increase in feelings of neglect or interference on the part of their families.

Employment and Economic Circumstances

Table 6 shows that in 1956, when the subjects were first interviewed, many men and women reported that they were still working, either full-time or part-time. Some farmers' wives considered themselves employed part-time if they participated in some of the farm work. A few men at the later interviews reported they were working, which reflects the status of some subjects who were "retired" farmers but still owned farms and helped manage them or work on them as needed.

In terms of chief sources of financial support—a question asked at all three interviews—the subjects' answers shifted somewhat from reliance upon their present earnings to a reliance upon Social Security, pensions, investments, and savings (Table 6). Reports of Old Age Assistance and relief remained few and stable over the years; some subjects said they were receiving aid from their children. No one indicated that he was receiving support solely from relief, Old Age Assistance, or from his children. The

TABLE 6

Employment Status and Economic Information on
Longitudinal Ss, by Percent

	Men			Women		
Item	1956	1962	1965	1956	1962	1965
Employment status (N)	(16)	(16)	(16)	(27)	(24)	(29)
Working full-time	50	13	6	44	0	0
Working part-time	31	19	13	52	13	3
Not working	19	69	81	4	88	97
Chief sources of support (N)	(17)	(16)	(17)	(28)	(27)	(27)
Present earnings (includes						
spouse's)	47	31	18	50	15	11
Social Security	53	88	82	32	63	67
Pension, earlier occupation	18	25	29	14	19	22
Investments, savings	41	25	53	39	33	57
Insurance, annuities	6	19	6	11	4	11
Old Age Assistance, relief	12	6	18	4	–	7
Aid from children	12	6	18	11	11	19
Other sources	12	6	6	11	22	15
Home ownership (N)	(17)	(16)	(14)	(28)	(27)	(27)
Yes, clear of indebtedness	76	81	93	75	78	67
Yes, still paying	6	–	–	4	–	4
No	18	19	8	21	22	30
Self-rating on economic						
position (N)	(17)	(16)	(17)	(29)	(27)	(29)
Well-to-do	–	6	–	4	4	–
Comfortable	63	44	40	43	56	54
Enough to get along	38	44	60	43	37	43
Can't make ends meet	–	6	–	11	4	4
Present economic position (N)	(17)	(16)	(14)	(27)	(27)	(28)
(In 1956, compared to age 55;						
in 1962, to 1956; in 1965, to						
1962)						
Better now	76	19	14	37	22	4
About the same	23	56	79	44	70	93
Worse now	–	25	7	19	7	4

common and highly valued pattern seemed to be modest living within one's own independent financial means, and a part of that pattern for almost all men, and for a majority of the women, included home ownership.

The subjects were also asked this question: "How would you describe your present (economic) position in life?" These replies are also shown in Table 6. Almost all subjects saw themselves as being "comfortable" or having "enough to get along," but some downward shifts occurred over the years with the men. When asked in 1956 to compare their circumstances with when they were aged 55, three-fourths of the men and one-third of the women said they were better off now. This probably reflects the fact that at that time in their middle age these men found themselves quite pressed to provide for their families during the Depression and felt better off now. Some were worse now, indeed, perhaps because of widowhood or retirement. In the other comparisons with the times we previously interviewed them, a majority of the participants said they were about the same now as before.

Friendships, Activities, and Religion

Table 7 provides additional descriptive information from the interviews. "How many friends would you say you have?" we asked them. "Oh, my!" many replied, and most responded with a number of ten or more. "How many are such close friends that you can talk to them about almost anything?" we then asked. Differences between men and women appeared here: considerably more men than women again replied that there were ten or more, while almost a third of the women said that none of them were.

TABLE 7

Friendships, Activities, and Religion of
Longitudinal Ss, by Percent

Item	Men			Women		
	1956	1962	1965	1956	1962	1965
Number of friends (N)	(15)	(15)	(14)	(28)	(27)	(29)
Ten or more	93	93	70	89	100	93
Five to nine	—	—	7	7	—	7
One to four	7	7	14	4	—	—
None	—	—	7	—	—	—

TABLE 7 (Continued)

Item	Men			Women		
	1956	*1962*	*1965*	*1956*	*1962*	*1965*
Number of close friends (N)	(11)	(10)	(12)	(25)	(23)	(26)
Ten or more	45	50	33	12	9	15
Five to nine	27	20	17	12	17	12
One to four	18	30	33	48	43	38
None	9	—	17	28	30	35
Number of free-time activities (N)	(17)	(16)	(15)	(28)	(27)	(29)
Seven or more	6	44	60	14	59	76
Three to six	23	50	33	32	41	21
One or two	59	6	—	36	—	3
Just sit and think	12	—	7	18	—	—
Frequency of attending club meetings (N)	(17)	(16)	(16)	(28)	(26)	(28)
Once a week or more	—	6	—	21	19	18
Once or twice a month	12	31	13	29	35	36
Less than once a month	23	6	13	18	15	14
Never	65	56	75	32	31	32
Time given to organizations (N)	(16)	(16)	(15)	(27)	(27)	(25)
(In 1956, compared to age 55; in 1962, to 1956; in 1965, to 1962)						
More now	13	—	—	33	15	—
About the same	38	88	67	37	67	56
Less now	50	13	33	30	19	44
Church membership[a] (N)	(17)	(16)	(15)	(28)	(27)	(28)
Yes	71	69	73	89	93	82
No	29	31	27	11	7	18
Frequency of attending church (N)	(17)	(16)	(17)	(28)	(27)	(29)
Once a week or more	41	50	29	61	56	52
Once or twice a month	6	—	—	11	11	3
Less than once a month	35	31	29	21	22	14
Never	18	19	41	7	11	31

[a] *Except for one man who defined his own religion, all Ss were Protestant.*

Still it is safe to say that our subjects were socially active persons who felt they had many friends, although the numbers with whom they were involved seemed to decrease over the years.

A list of some twenty activities was read to the interviewee following this query: "What do you do in your free time?" The list included such activities as working in and around the house, working in the garden and yard, watching TV, writing letters, attending concerts, playing golf, taking rides, visiting friends, or "just sitting and thinking." The numbers of these were tallied and, as shown in Table 7, the number which both men and women listed over the years, exclusive of replying "just sitting and thinking" increased. Over the same period, it will be recalled, the number of subjects who were employed decreased so that more free time was presumably available. During the same period there was some fluctuation in the number of club meetings the men and women attended; from 1956 to 1962 a slight increase, and for the men a slight decrease from 1962 to 1965. This is also shown by the comparative information in Table 7.

Almost all the women, and certainly majorities of the men, were church members (all except one being Protestant and, incidentally, all white); majorities of women said they attended once a week or more often, with fewer men in this category. More men than women said they never attended, and for both sexes this number increased over the nine-year period of the study.

Evaluation of Happiness and Accomplishments

Table 8 provides the responses of men and women to this question: "As you look back over your life, in general would you call it very happy, moderately happy, average, or unhappy?" Generally there was not much difference between the men and women; over half evaluated their lives as moderately or very happy. At the third assessment point a few said their lives were unhappy.

Asked how they felt about what they had accomplished in life, nine out of ten subjects said they were reasonably satisfied or well satisfied. These men and women were not given to effervescing about themselves and their accomplishments, so these responses, changing little over the years, seem to fit them well. A few stated that they were dissatisfied with what they had accomplished.

The data presented thus far concern items from the interviews which show some change and some stability of the subjects as groups. Let us turn now to the measures of personality and adjustment used at the three points of assessment.

TABLE 8

Evaluations of Happiness and Accomplishments in Life,
Longitudinal Ss, by Percent

	Men			Women		
Item	1956	1962	1965	1956	1962	1965
Self-rating of happiness in						
life (N)	(17)	(16)	(16)	(28)	(27)	(29)
Very happy	18	13	25	36	22	10
Moderately happy	35	44	25	25	33	52
Average	47	44	44	39	44	31
Unhappy	—	—	6	—	—	7
Feelings about accomplishments						
(N)	(17)	(14)	(16)	(28)	(27)	(29)
Well satisfied	35	21	19	43	22	28
Reasonably satisfied	59	64	81	54	74	69
Dissatisfied	6	14	—	4	4	3

PERSONALITY AND ADJUSTMENT AT THREE POINTS IN TIME

The Three Measurements

Several measures of personality and adjustment were used to assess the subjects at three points in time. These measures have already been described, and in Tables 9-13 data on each measure are presented for the men and women as groups. In addition, inter-year correlations are presented for each measure. Particular attention is given to differences between men and women and to differences between the groups as measured in 1956, 1962, and 1965.

The distributions of scores on the Activity Inventory are shown in Table 9. For men and women the scores were concentrated in the middle portions of the distribution, and the ranges increased over time, especially for the men. From the mean scores it appears that the scores of both men and women decreased over the years, indicating less overt activity on their part. According to the average deviations (showing the extent to which, on the average, subjects differ from the mean scores) and the ranges, the men increased in variability more than the women.

TABLE 9

Activity and Attitude Inventory Scores for Longitudinal
Ss, by Percent

Measure, Score, Statistic	Men			Women		
	1956	1962	1965	1956	1962	1965
Activity Inventory[a] (N)	(17)	(17)	(16)	(28)	(28)	(28)
45-49	—	—	6	11	—	—
40-44	6	18	—	7	18	14
35-39	47	29	13	21	32	21
30-34	35	23	44	43	21	32
25-29	—	12	6	4	21	18
24 or less	12	18	31	14	7	14
Range	20-41	18-44	16-45	22-48	17-44	17-42
Mean	32.24	32.29	29.50	33.93	33.04	31.64
Average Deviation	3.34	6.00	6.00	5.29	5.18	5.14
Attitude Inventory[b] (N)	(16)	(17)	(13)	(29)	(28)	(28)
45-48	13	—	—	3	4	—
40-44	38	18	23	38	25	14
35-39	25	35	23	41	50	54
30-34	13	23	39	7	11	29
25-29	13	6	15	7	7	4
24 or less	—	18	—	3	4	—
Range	27-47	16-44	25-43	24-45	14-45	29-44
Mean	38.19	33.59	34.54	37.93	36.61	36.21
Average Deviation	4.66	5.82	3.96	3.78	3.96	2.79

[a]Total possible score = 60.
[b]Total possible score = 48.

On the Attitude Inventory, for both men and women the mean scores were lower at the last point compared to the first, as were the average deviations. The proportions of men and women in the upper categories decreased, while the proportions in the middle categories increased over the years.

When judges rated interview material and made evaluations of adjustment in terms of primary relationships, emotional security, etc., women were rated higher, on the average, than men, and as a group they varied from each other more than did the men. Proportionally more women were in the upper categories all three years, but there were increases in the proportions of men and women who received lower ratings with time. Comparing the mean scores for the Judge's Rating for 1956 and 1965, the latter were considerably lower (Table 10).

Using a combined adaptation of Guilford and Zimmerman's Personal Relations and Sociability Scales with our subjects (Table 10), we found few differences between the men and women consistently appearing over the years. Women varied somewhat more from each other at the first and last points in the analysis, as shown by the ranges and the average deviations.

Table 11 shows data for the Thematic Apperception Test. (On the TAT the responses of considerably fewer subjects in 1965

TABLE 10

Judge's Rating and Personal Relations—
Sociability Scores for Longitudinal Ss,
by Percent

Measure, Score, Statistic	Men			Women		
	1956	1962	1965	1956	1962	1965
Judge's Rating[a] (N)	(17)	(17)	(17)	(28)	(28)	(29)
35 or more	6	12	—	29	25	3
30-34	12	18	6	18	21	21
25-29	41	35	29	25	25	10
20-24	29	29	41	14	21	48
19 or less	12	6	24	14	7	17
Range	15-37	18-37	12-30	9-42	17-40	15-37
Mean	25.35	27.06	22.77	28.11	29.43	24.07
Average Deviation	3.67	4.24	3.56	6.85	5.74	4.07
Personal Relations and Sociability Scale[b] (N)	(17)	(17)	(13)	(29)	(28)	(28)
20-22	—	—	8	10	7	18
17-19	35	29	15	28	21	18
14-16	41	23	46	41	46	43
11-13	23	29	23	10	18	11
10 or less	—	18	8	10	7	11
Range	11-18	8-18	10-20	9-21	9-20	6-20
Mean	15.12	13.71	14.85	15.59	14.96	15.36
Average Deviation	1.66	2.78	2.53	2.54	2.04	2.89

[a]Total possible score = 54.
[b]Total possible score = 23.

could be evaluated, as we have explained earlier.) The mean scores of the men increased, as did their average deviations. Greater proportions of men were in the highest two categories at the latter points in the study, and greater proportions of women were in the lowest categories at all three points.

TABLE 11

Thematic Apperception Test and Opinion Conformity Scale
Scores for Longitudinal Ss, by Percent

Measure, Score, Statistic	Men			Women		
	1956	1962	1965	1956	1962	1965
Thematic Apperception Test[a] (N)	(16)	(17)	(9)	(26)	(28)	(19)
450 or above	–	6	22	4	7	5
425-449	13	35	33	31	25	11
400-424	56	53	22	27	18	47
375-399	25	6	11	35	29	37
374 or less	6	–	11	4	21	–
Range	336-431	392-472	373-481	356-450	319-468	383-500
Mean	401.75	442.94	424.33	409.19	403.39	412.35
Average Deviation	14.38	12.88	24.30	20.67	27.28	18.71
Opinion Conformity Scale[b] (N)	(17)	(17)	(14)	(28)	(28)	(27)
12	12	–	14	36	32	11
11	12	41	14	21	25	26
10	23	29	21	32	25	33
9	35	29	43	11	11	19
8	18	–	7	–	8	11
Range	8-12	9-11	8-12	9-12	7-12	7-12
Mean	9.65	10.12	9.68	10.82	10.61	10.04
Average Deviation	1.03	.72	1.00	.92	1.09	.92

[a]Total possible score = 714.
[b]Total possible score = 12.

On the Opinion Conformity Scale (Table 11), the higher the score the greater the degree of conformity to norms for old people within the community. More women than men received high scores at all three assessment points, although the means were not much different. The variability of both men and women was quite limited.

The Reputation Ratings for the longitudinal subjects, obtained in the community-wide survey of 1955, are shown in Table 12. Forty-one percent of the men and 28 percent of the women were not mentioned as outstanding in one way or another in that survey, but over one-third of both men and women were mentioned positively (5-7 ratings). A few were mentioned negatively. The average male reputation rating was about the same as the average for females.

TABLE 12

Reputation Ratings (1955) for Longitudinal Ss, by Percent

Measure, Score, Statistic	Men	Women
Reputation Rating[a] (N)	(17)	(29)
Not mentioned	41	28
7 (High)	6	17
6	6	—
5	23	21
4	18	17
3 or below (Low)	6	17
Range	3-7	2-7
Mean	4.80	4.71
Average Deviation	.84	1.25

[a]Total possible score = 7.

Interviewers were in a position to rate the interviewees on several important dimensions in terms of personality functioning, including their ability to give the interview attention and to interact and cooperate in that situation (Table 13). In the first year of assessment the ratings seem especially high, particularly for the women. The comparative reference points for using the five-point scales were not defined in any absolute sense, but obviously the women fared better than men on such ratings. The means decreased for men and women over the years, indicating somewhat lessened functional ability; the greatest dispersion of ratings showed up in 1965.

TABLE 13

Interviewer's Ratings for Longitudinal Ss, by Percent

Measure, Score, Statistic	Men			Women		
	1956	1962	1965	1956	1962	1965
Interviewer's Rating[a] (N)	(17)	(17)	(16)	(29)	(28)	(29)
29-30	23	—	—	62	18	10
27-28	23	12	19	21	18	10
25-26	12	23	31	3	14	28
23-24	18	12	—	10	21	10
21-22	18	18	19	3	11	17
19-20	—	23	13	—	14	21
17 or below	6	12	19	—	4	3
Range	16-30	13-28	15-28	21-30	13-30	14-30
Mean	25.41	23.06	22.75	28.41	24.43	23.72
Average Deviation	3.32	4.31	3.50	1.90	3.43	3.06

[a]Total possible score = 30.

The Community Ratings are discussed in Chapter 5.

TABLE 14

Community Rating Scores for Longitudinal Q-Subjects
Only[a], by Percent

Measure, Score, Statistic	1956	1962	1965
Community Rating[b] (N)	(14)	(14)	(14)
130-149	7	7	14
110-129	29	14	14
90-109	21	36	14
70-89	29	36	36
50-69	14	7	21
Range	65-148	71-137	59-134
Mean	96.14	93.86	91.07
Average Deviation	21.77	18.86	20.39

[a]Includes three men and eleven women; these Q Ss are included in other longitudinal subject analyses.
[b]Total possible score = 150.

Inter-Year Correlations

For comparisons of the measures between and among the years, we have presented distributions of scores for the men and women for all three points of assessment. To determine the extent to which the *ranking* of individuals on the measures at one point corresponded to their ranking at a later point, we calculated *inter-year correlations.* This method permitted us to determine how predictable the men and women as groups were over varying intervals of time—six years (1956 to 1962), three years (1962 to 1965), or nine years (1956 to 1965). These inter-year correlations are presented in Table 15.

It might have been expected that one could predict change more easily over a short term than over a long term, and these data provide a test of this hypothesis. One might qualify that hypothesis, however, and posit that the impact of events in individuals' lives might be expected to differ according to when, developmentally, those events occurred within their own life histories.

Except for a very few, all the correlations are low, and rather little variance could be explained by the relationships. All except two were positive. Men do differ from women; the inter-year correlations are generally higher for men than for women. Except for the Community Rating, the higher correlations are with those three measures which are loaded on an activity factor (Britton, 1963), especially the Activity Inventory, the Attitude Inventory, and the Judge's Rating.

In general, as shown by inter-year correlation coefficients, however, there was little consistency of the subjects in relation to each other over time. The time period with the most correlations that were statistically significant was, as we hypothesized, the shortest period of time—from 1962 to 1965; the longer time spans 1956-1962 and 1956-1965, contained fewer significant correlations. Generally, the correlations did not vary much according to the difference in time or age (or developmental) span; we could have predicted as well, or as poorly, for a nine-year span as we could have for a three-year or a six-year span at the particular points in the life cycles of our subjects.

There were few, if any, consistent differences between the so-called objective measures (the Activity and Attitude inventories, the P and S Scale, and the Opinion Conformity Scale) and the

TABLE 15

Correlations[a] of Measures Between Years of Assessment for the 17 Men and 29 Women Longitudinal Ss and 14 Q-Subjects[b]

Measure and Group	Time Period		
	1956-62	1962-65	1956-65
Activity Inventory			
Men	70	69	72
Women	65	53	53
Attitude Inventory			
Men	41	89	59
Women	40	36	−06
Judge's Rating			
Men	33	63	57
Women	70	60	56
Personal Relations and Sociability Test			
Men	48	50	61
Women	35	50	41
Thematic Apperception Test			
Men	26	52	21
Women	53	27	42
Opinion Conformity Scale			
Men	−19	01	03
Women	30	41	30
Interviewer's Rating			
Men	27	63	63
Women	15	26	49
Community Rating			
Q only (men and women)	93	96	90

[a]Pearson product-moment correlations; decimals are omitted. To be statistically significant, r must be .48 for 17 men, .36 for 29 women, and .53 for the 14 Q-subjects.
[b]N's vary slightly among measures because of unscorable measures.

more subjective measures (the Judge's and Interviewer's ratings, the Community Rating, and the TAT).

INDIVIDUAL CHANGE OVER TIME

Thus far we have examined data concerning continuity and change of our men and women subjects *as groups*. A major interest, however, was in *individual* change or consistency over the years of the study. One means by which individual change can be shown is by use of individual change profiles, and we shall later describe some individuals in this way by means of abbreviated case studies. To be able to evaluate change on a more systematic basis, we used the Longitudinal Trend Score (LTS), interpreted, as we have explained, like a correlation coefficient showing direction and degree of individual change over the nine-year period.

Change Data

Tables 16-19 present distributions of Longitudinal Trend Scores for the men and women for the various measures and for a mean LTS. In the presentations we have arbitrarily divided the distributions into thirds, that is, those +.50 and higher, indicating rather marked positive change (improvement) over the years; —.49 to +.49, signifying no real change (maintenance); and —.50 and higher, showing rather marked negative change (decline) over the years of the research. We also provide the range, mean, and average deviation for each LTS measure.

For the Activity Inventory (Table 16), about one-fifth of the men and women changed upwardly over the nine-year period of the study, but proportionally more men than women changed for the worse. The mean LTS was negative for both men and women, although in the no-change category. The range was wide for both, with the average deviation about the same for both men and women.

On the Attitude Inventory, two-thirds of the men and slightly fewer women declined over the years, a few did not change at all, and one-fourth to one-third changed positively. The mean LTS was negative for both, and women varied somewhat more widely from the average than did men.

With the Judge's Rating, again the mean LTS was negative, and again the range was wide. Substantial proportions of both men and women were in the negative change category. About one-fifth of the subjects had changed for the better, however. Quite a number had not changed at all (Table 16).

On the P and S Scale (Table 17), mean LTS scores were

TABLE 16

Longitudinal Trend Scores for Activity and Attitude Inventories
and Judge's Rating, Longitudinal Ss, by Percent

Measure, Score, Statistic	Men	Women
Activity Inventory (N)	(16)	(25)
+.50 and higher +	19	20
−.49 to +.49	31	40
−.50 and higher −	50	40
Range	−.99 to +.90	−.99 to +.94
Mean	−.39	−.22
Average Deviation	.51	.48
Attitude Inventory (N)	(12)	(26)
+.50 and higher +	25	31
−.49 to +.49	8	12
−.50 and higher −	67	58
Range	−.98 to +.88	−.99 to +.98
Mean	−.38	−.25
Average Deviation	.63	.75
Judge's Rating (N)	(16)	(26)
+.50 and higher +	19	23
−.49 to +.49	38	19
−.50 and higher −	44	58
Range	−.99 to +.99	−1.00 to +1.00
Mean	−.25	−.30
Average Deviation	.57	.57

negative but showed little change. More men than women were in the no-change category, and more women than men on this measure had changed for the worse over the nine-year period.

We have already noted difficulties in administering the TAT to our subjects, and reduction in N's of these LTS scores was noted. As we have said, the TAT stories were evaluated in terms of how adequate the subjects saw the older person in the stories. These mean LTS's were two of the few positive ones revealed in the analysis. The findings show that men scored higher than women on this measure. The means reflect this difference, as does the fact that seven out of ten men and nearly five out of ten women improved on this measure. Quite a number did not change, but over one-third of the women declined on this measure. Nevertheless there were wide individual differences.

Scores on the Opinion Conformity Scale LTS's (Table 17) for one-quarter of the subjects increased over the period of the study; this actually meant that they became more conforming to the predominant culture of the area, as shown on this twelve-item scale. One-half of the women and one-third of the men became less conforming according to this measure. The average LTS was negative, in the no-change category, but the variability of the group was fairly wide.

TABLE 17

Longitudinal Trend Scores for Personal Relations and Sociability Scale, TAT, and Opinion Conformity Scale, Longitudinal Ss, by Percent

Measure, Score, Statistic	Men	Women
Personal Relations and Sociability Scale (N)	(13)	(26)
+.50 and higher +	23	31
+.49 and −.49	46	27
−.50 and higher −	31	42
Range	−.99 to +.75	−1.00 to +1.00
Mean	−.19	−.13
Average Deviation	.45	.63
Thematic Apperception Test (N)	(10)	(19)
+.50 and higher +	70	47
+.49 to −.49	20	16
−.50 and higher −	10	37
Range	−.68 to +.99	−.99 to +.99
Mean	.53	.07
Average Deviation	.28	.73
Opinion Conformity Scale (N)	(12)	(23)
+.50 and higher +	25	26
+.49 to −.49	42	22
−.50 and higher −	33	52
Range	−.98 to +.94	−.99 to +.94
Mean	−.35	−.26
Average Deviation	.69	.64

Table 18 provides the LTS's for the Interviewer's Rating, which included evaluations of the interviewee's ability to see, hear, and interact. No woman and only two men were seen as improving on this measure. The great majority, about three-fourths, declined in these functional abilities, as was seen in the interview situation. The mean change was negative, markedly so for the women, and variability was relatively limited.

The Community Rating was for the Q-group subjects and will be discussed in Chapter 5.

TABLE 18

Longitudinal Trend Scores for Interviewer's Rating and
Community Rating, Longitudinal Ss, by Percent

Measure, Score, Statistic	Men	Women
Interviewer's Rating (N)	(16)	(28)
+.50 and higher +	13	—
−.49 to +.49	19	21
−.50 and higher −	69	79
Range	−1.00 to +.94	−1.00 to −.09
Mean	−.43	−.74
Average Deviation	.47	.22
Community Rating for Q's (N)	(3)	(11)
+.50 and higher +	67	9
−.49 to +.49	—	18
−.50 and higher −	33	73
Range	−.91 to +.94	−1.00 to +.65
Mean	.32	−.61
Average Deviation	.82	.39

A Mean Longitudinal Trend Score was derived in order to show how much, on the average, subjects changed on the measures of personality and adjustment, not including the Community Rating (Table 19). No subject appeared in the markedly positive change categories of +.50 or higher, but one-fifth of the men and over one-third of the women appeared in the markedly negative change categories. The highest positive trend persons were still in our no-change category (−.49 to +.49); in fact, 78 percent of the men and 62 percent of the women were, according to the average

LTS, stable or maintaining themselves on our measures. There were still several subjects whose average LTS's showed marked positive change—three men and ten women.

Averages, of course, summarize in a gross way the variations inherent in individuals and the measures. The LTS's were more or less independent of each other, as might be expected from the conceptual and operational bases of the measures. This is true, with the exception that the measures which themselves are intercorrelated (the Activity Inventory, Attitude Inventory, and Judge's Rating) also appear to be associated when it comes to a change analysis.

TABLE 19

Mean Longitudinal Trend Scores, Longitudinal Ss, by Percent

Measure, Score, Statistic	Men	Women
Mean LTS (N)[a]	(14)[a]	(27)[a]
+.25 to +.49	21	7
+.00 to +.24	—	11
−.01 to −.24	14	22
−.25 to −.49	43	22
−.50 to −.74	21	33
−.75 to −.99	—	4
Range	−.72 to +.44	−.76 to +.37
Mean	−.20	−.25
Average Deviation	.31	.27

[a]Calculated only for those Ss having four or more of the seven measures available, not counting Community Rating.

Factors Associated with Change

The analyses so far presented are attempts to delineate the extent to which individuals changed during a nine-year period in later maturity and old age. We were also interested in what factors tended to be associated with change. Since the LTS's ranged from positive to negative, we divided our subjects simply according to whether they changed on a given measure in a positive direction or in a negative one, and then used Fisher's Exact Probability Test or chi-square (Siegel, 1956)—whichever was appropriate. In some instances frequencies were too few in some statistical cells for either test to be used.

Thus we determined the statistical significance of differences between the positive change group and the negative change group for the LTS's included in Tables 16-19. These analyses were made for the sexes separately, except for those involving the Community Rating, when the men and women subjects were combined. The results are not presented in table form but follow here:

One series of analyses included the following variables measured in 1956: age, education, occupational status of family wage earner, present employment status, home ownership, number of leisure activities, and frequency of church attendance. Only one such comparison was of statistical significance at the five percent or less than five percent level: significantly more women than expected, among those who changed positively on the Judge's Rating, attended church less than once per week.

In another series of analyses, the following 1956 self-ratings were used: health status, economic position, happiness in marriage, accomplishments in life, and happiness in life. For men, significantly more than expected of those who had rated their health as good or excellent in 1956 declined over the years on the Personal Relations and Sociability Test. For women, significantly more than expected of those who rated their health in 1956 as good or excellent declined on the Judge's Rating over the years of the study; further, significantly more than expected of those women who rated their marriage as having been happy or very happy (in contrast to average or unhappy) declined over the years on the Activity Inventory and on the Mean Longitudinal Trend Score.

In a third series of analyses, the Reputation Rating of 1955 and the two scores derived from the WAIS Similarities Test administered in 1965 were used. No significant differences appeared for women subjects, but for male subjects those who scored relatively high on the WAIS Similarities raw (15 or higher) and the age-scaled scores (20 or higher) in 1965 tended to have improved their standing on the Judge's Rating over the years of the investigation.

Thus, our investigation contributes little helpful information of a statistical nature to delineate factors associated with change in one direction or another in our longitudinal subjects. This general finding seems to be corroborated in the case study analysis we have made of individuals, to which we turn now.

Some Individual "Changers" and "Nonchangers"

To provide an opportunity to look at continuity and change in personality and adjustment as a personal and social process, we have selected several men and women whose interviews, tests, and records were examined carefully on an individual basis. Some cases were chosen on the basis of their exemplifying subjects in the study who declined on most of the measures over the years. Others were chosen because they maintained themselves or even improved their status on the measures. They are not necessarily typical of others, but others may be similar to them in a number of ways. A number of details have been changed to protect their anonymity.

Improver-Maintainer

Mr. H.

Mr. H., who was 69 years old when we first met him in 1956, was married and living with his wife in their own home. His marital status did not change, nor did his living arrangements over the course of the study. Mr. H. had worked all his life as a laborer, and although he was not gainfully employed when we first knew him, he accepted a full-time custodial position in 1962 and was continuing with it in 1965. He had attended an ungraded school but did not remember at what age he had left school.

Mr. H. rated his physical health as fair to good; and never, during the years we talked to him, did he report any days spent in bed. He could think of no serious physical problems that were troublesome but did say that feelings of tiredness, aching joints, and belching were some difficulties he occasionally experienced. Indeed, on two occasions he mentioned his good health as an important advantage to him in growing older.

In terms of activities, we found that over the years (from age 69 to age 78) Mr. H. increased the number of activities he pursued—and this, it must be remembered, was when he was also employed full-time. He managed to engage in a wide variety of activities ranging from house and garden work to TV watching, visiting, and playing with grandchildren to helping with civic and fire hall activities. He maintained his church membership over the years and attended regularly, helping with as many church-related activities as he could.

One of the roles which Mr. H. was reported to play vigorously was his role as father of eight children and grandparent of many more. On several independent occasions the interviewer remarked on the close-knit quality of his immediate and extended family. Mr. H. was thoroughly pleased and satisfied with the success and happiness of his children and also with his own, although he rather realistically expressed his feelings that things could have been a "little better and a little worse" for him. He did show some concern, but not overconcern, with his financial situation, especially with respect to the effects a long or severe illness could have. (The study began before Social Security coverage or any type of public medical care program was typically available to our subjects.) Mr. H. managed to maintain, and apparently to thrive on, a careful and frugal style of living.

In his interaction with the interviewers, Mr. H. was described as pleasant and kindly. "He's a wonderful old man with a good sense of humor," one said. He was matter-of-fact in answering the questions and modestly volunteered little additional information about himself. He appeared to have a quality of inner stability and confidence in himself and his place in life. Sometimes he appeared to feel unsure of his answers, and in fact at one point saw as a disadvantage of aging his not being able to keep up with "thinking and stuff like that."

On all the regular measures of personality and adjustment we used, he scored above the mean at all three points in time. Four of his Longitudinal Trend Scores were high and positive and, according to our criteria, classified him as an "improver"; two other Longitudinal Trend Scores place him in our "maintainer" category. We see him, then, as one who, over the nine years of the study—from age 69 to 78—maintained himself or improved himself on our measurements. On the WAIS Similarities his age-scaled score of 8 was below the mean of 10.23 for the longitudinal men. In terms of his "reputation" in the community *in 1956*, he was not mentioned, in either positive or negative terms.

Improver-Maintainer

Mr. T.

Mr. T. was 64 years old when our study began and was still gainfully employed as a civil servant in a position he had held for 39 years. In his younger days, he had served in the army and he had also taught school for a time. He was married and lived in his own home with his wife, and they were the parents of one son. At the last point in the study, in 1965, Mr. T. had been widowed the previous year but, although now alone, he continued to live in the same residence.

In 1956 Mr. T. was beginning to be concerned about his physical health, having undergone prostate gland surgery, and he described his health as "fair." In 1962 he felt his health had improved since we had previously seen him although his problems still included poor sight and hearing and heart trouble. He reported that he had been forced to spend two weeks in bed during the previous year (when he was 70) after falling off his tractor while working on his farm. Mr. T. rated his health in 1965 as good—no days were spent in bed; he listed his poor sight and hearing as being "slight" problems to him.

Mr. T. participated in many community organizations, including the volunteer fire company, a veterans' organization, a Golden Age Club, and a lodge. He said that he saw himself as *both* a "social type" *and* an "at-home type." At the beginning of the study, Mr. T. reported that he had almost no free time, since he was working, whereas by 1962 he had increased his nonworking activities. In addition to his work around the house and garden, plus work on his farm outside town, he attended meetings on schedule, went visiting, did some entertaining, and also drove race horses.

Mr. T. impressed us as being pleased with himself and his accomplishments sometimes to the point of wanting to impress others, especially with his economic success. He appeared to enjoy the functions of giving advice to others from his store of fairly strong opinions and viewpoints. We suspected that he liked to dominate social situations in a gentle way and to "run things."

To our interviewers, he was cheerful, pleasant, and talkative. During our last interview with him he openly spoke of his extreme loneliness after the death of his wife, and he seemed eager for social contact and to be of assistance to anyone in any way he could. He recalled with pleasure his previous participation in the study and inquired about the persons who had interviewed him then.

On our measures of personality and adjustment, Mr. T. scored at or below the mean at our first assessment and generally above the mean at the latter two points. In 1965 his age-scaled score on the WAIS Similarities Scale was 11, above the mean for our men. He was well-known in the community, and was favorably seen by those who mentioned him in our study of reputations. He was also known by our panelists and happened to have been selected for the Community Rating, on which his relative standing was well below the mean—in fact, over an average deviation below.

As to trends over time, five of Mr. T.'s Longitudinal Trend Scores were high and positive—in our "improver" category; a sixth was in the zero range; the seventh showed marked decline.

Decliner

Mr. Z.

At the beginning of our study Mr. Z. was a 67-year-old man, married and living with his wife and son. His marital status remained the same throughout the time we knew him. He had attended "normal school" until he was 18 and had spent most of his working years farming; he and his wife had reared eight children. During the entire study period, however, Mr. Z. was not gainfully employed.

In 1956 Mr. Z. indicated by his comments that he felt himself to be in good health but troubled by such problems as hernia, arthritis, and gas pains. In 1962 these problems persisted, with the additional ones of poor hearing and shortness of breath; he rated his health as "fair" and as worse than when we had seen him earlier. When we saw him in 1965, Mr. Z. rated himself in good health, believing his health to have improved since 1962. He then added poor sight and feelings of tiredness to his previous physical difficulties.

Over the years of the study Mr. Z told us that he belonged to no clubs or organizations and indeed, though he identified himself as a Protestant at our first meeting and as a Lutheran at our last, he consistently said he was not a church *member*.

Concerning his leisure time activities from 1956 to 1965, Mr. Z. revealed few, and those were mainly sedentary and often solitary ones, such as TV watching. He initially revealed another aspect of himself when he reported that sleeping was one of his activities, which suggested that at 67 years of age he may have found it useful to escape from the circumstances around him. His activity seemed to have decreased markedly over the years, and more of his time to have been filled with "just sitting and thinking." Difficulties in hearing and seeing probably were important in isolating him further, but perhaps in an involuntary way. He seems to have been "disengaged" and "disengaging" for a number of years (Cumming and Henry, 1961).

In 1956 the interviewer felt that Mr. Z. was a dissatisfied and insecure person who had a negative attitude toward people and who thought his life had *not* been particularly enjoyable. He seemed to reply to the questions in a tone that expressed amusement, but the interviewer felt that this was his way of concealing his true feelings about things that were relevant, meaningful, or frightening to him. He and his wife "warmed" considerably as the interview progressed, according to the interviewer, who described the house and farm as a "mess," and Mr. Z. and his wife as unclean looking. This could be interpreted as extensions of feelings about the "self."

In the 1962 interview situation, Mr. Z. was described as being defensive and openly and assertively opinionated. At that time he especially disliked questions concerning his friendships and claimed to have none.

In 1965 Mr. Z. felt himself to be in better physical health, but he appeared to be concerned over his financial situation. He was also critical of the amount of affection and attention he was receiving.

Throughout our contact with him, Mr. Z. seemed to function intellectually at an average level, being particularly well-informed about current events and national politics. He refused, however, to be evaluated by means of the WAIS Similarities Scale, which may indicate something of his own concern about his adequacy. When he was mentioned in our study of reputations, it was in a negative manner.

On the other measures we used, he was scored well below the mean at all three points of assessment. This was true except for the Opinion Conformity Scale; on that he was above the mean, showing above-average agreement with community norms for old people. As to trends over the nine years, five of his six Longitudinal Trend Scores showed definite decline; the sixth Longitudinal Trend Score was in our no-change category.

Decliner

Mr. D.

We first came to know Mr. D. in 1956, when he was 66 years old, married and living with his wife, and still working as a second-level elected county official. The job was confining but he was partially compensated for it by the county's providing him with living quarters. He reported that he had completed eight grades of school and had at one time been employed as a steward at the county home, and that he had engaged in farming off and on. He and his wife were the parents of five children.

Through the years Mr. D. consistently reported that he felt his health to be only "fair," although no serious problems plagued him and although over the nine-year period of our contact with him he could recall no days spent sick in bed. Reports from interviewers at all three periods in time verified his self-report that he was in good health; at one point (1956) the interviewer remarked that Mr. D. did not look his years, and still later in the study he was described as being "alert and active and obviously in good health."

At the same time, however, Mr. D. complained casually of shortness of breath, aching joints, and a tired feeling. When we consider that most of his life Mr. D. had by choice been in situations in which he was called upon to be physically vigorous and active, these ailments may have had more meaning for him than they would have had for some others.

After Mr. D.'s term in office expired, he and his wife moved from the house the county provided to a home of their own. They occupied this home together until Mrs. D. died in 1963. Mr. D. mentioned that owning his own home and being free from debt was one of the advantages he enjoyed as he grew older. At the time of his wife's death, Mr. D. moved across town to live with his daughter and her family. Again the interviewer reported that, on the surface at least, Mr. D. had accepted his wife's death and seemed to be adjusting well.

Over the nine-year period, Mr. D. moved from the position of full-time work and having almost no free time at his disposal—yet managing to spend time working around the house and yard, gardening, shopping, visiting, and entertaining—to one in which he had all day free and filling it with the same activities as before. In 1962, however, he added that he did spend time "just sitting and thinking." This passive (depressive?), inwardly oriented activity was also mentioned in 1965. At no time were clubs or organized social activities of interest to him, but he must have been somewhat active politically and reasonably well regarded.

We got the impression from the interviewer's report that Mr. D. held his own as far as his *public* image was concerned. He was seen as a "good conversationalist, a thoroughly delightful person with a strong personality and a good sense of humor." He expressed satisfaction with his children's happiness and success, as well as with his own. At the same time, although activity was maintained, it was maintained in someone else's home and did not seem to carry the same meaning it once did. We sensed some covert self-dissatisfaction as well as hidden concern about his own death. He mentioned in 1962 that the main disadvantage of being his age (72) was just that life became shorter and shorter. Later, Mr. D. changed his church membership from one Protestant denomination to another; possibly he was "shopping around" for deeper meanings in his own life, or possibly new comfort patterns were needed.

On our measures of personality and adjustment, Mr. D. was generally somewhat above the means at all three points of assessment. On the WAIS Similarities Scale, his age-scaled score was 7 while the mean for our men was 10.23. Except for one Longitudinal Trend Score, the LTS's for Mr. D. all indicated marked negative change over the years of the study. He was not mentioned at all in our study of reputations of older persons in the community.

Maintainer-Improver

Mrs. A.

When we first met Mrs. A. in 1956, she was 77 years old, widowed, and living with her only son and his family, a living pattern that continued throughout the nine years we were in contact with her. As a child, Mrs. A. had completed eighth grade.

She and her husband had lived on a small farm which they operated; in addition, he worked on the county road as a laborer. Mrs. A. was not working gainfully when we knew her, and for the most part she had never worked outside the home during her adult years. As she put it, "I was content to care for my husband and son and I always enjoyed my home and garden."

One of the things Mrs. A was most proud of was her health, which she described as good. Over the years we knew her, she reported to us that she never spent a day in bed due to sickness. Her main health concerns in 1956, 1962, and 1965 were poor sight and hearing, but these problems did not, at least in terms of her own evaluation, worsen over the period. Difficulties of lesser magnitude included stiffness, gas pains and belching, constipation, and some feelings of tiredness. However, in 1965, when she was 86 years old, Mrs. A. checked none of the health problems except poor hearing and poor sight.

Although at all three assessment periods Mrs. A. explained to us that she had all day free to do as she pleased, she maintained a busy life concerned largely with activities around her home and garden and her son's family. She enjoyed making rugs, knitting, crocheting, taking rides with the family, and walking in the woods. TV and radio listening were winter activities she engaged in only when she could not get outdoors. Mrs. A. did not appear to be interested in clubs or organizations, and confided that she "just never got used to doing things like that." Mrs. A. was not affiliated with any church as a church member although she said she was Protestant and attended various churches in the community.

Although she did not dwell upon it or mention it as a disadvantage in growing older, Mrs. A. revealed in 1956 that her financial situation was grave and that she was economically dependent upon her son for most of her needs. However, interviewers at three points in time gained the impression that one reason Mrs. A. appeared to experience little guilt or unhappiness about this situation was because her son and daughter-in-law accepted it easily and Mrs. A. was indeed welcome in their home.

In Mrs. A.'s interaction with interviewers she was described as being pleasant, attractive, well-kept, and in good spirits. At age 86, when we saw her last, she was still "very active, in excellent health, pleasant, with a good sense of humor."

On the measures we employed in the research, Mrs. A.'s scores varied considerably—some being above and some close to or below the mean. Over the years the Longitudinal Trend Scores were definitely upward in four of the measures (Attitude Inventory, Judge's Rating, P and S, and TAT), rather stable for the Activity Inventory and Interviewer's Ratings, and downward for the Opinion Conformity Scale. Her Reputation Rating for 1955 was moderately positive. The WAIS Similarities scaled score was 0, indicating failure on all items given.

Maintainer

Miss C.

Miss C. impressed us when we first interviewed her at age 73 as being a stern, cold, harsh woman who lived in a shabby old house. She had never married and had lived alone all her life. After leaving school at age 15, when "the last book I had was an eighth grade reader," Miss C. worked in a factory and later as a domestic worker in local households.

Although Miss C. enumerated a number of physical problems and difficulties and constantly complained of things "getting on her nerves," she spent no days in bed during the nine years we knew her. Indeed, Miss C. valued her good health as a decided advantage to her. There were indications that she had difficulties in social relationships, and she volunteered the information that she had suffered a nervous breakdown at age 61.

Miss C. spent her days working around the house and yard and in church and Sunday School activities. Her activities included social as well as solitary pursuits.

One of the dominating characteristics in Miss C.'s life seemed to be her strong desire to remain self-sufficient and economically independent, despite the fact that her source of income was $40 per month from Social Security. She was proud of being able to be her "own boss" and gave every indication that she intended to stay that way. Among her stronger attitudes and opinions, three constantly recurred in the interviews: (1) an absolute and total rejection of receiving public assistance or support, (2) a rejection of any opinion or influence which she perceived to be imposed upon her by her nieces and nephews, and (3) an intense dislike of government tax policies, which she felt to be unjust.

In 1956 Miss C. was reported by the interviewer to reflect a generally bitter attitude toward, and mistrust of, other people; she expressed the feeling that she "would not tell any of her secrets to anyone." However, over the years we knew her, Miss C. continued to cooperate with the study and during our last interview she was described as being well-adjusted to her overall living situation and satisfied with it. As a matter of fact, though she refused to respond to the more structured aspects of the interview and the WAIS Similarities evaluation, she talked quite freely and in a fairly friendly fashion with the interviewer.

Miss C. might easily be seen as unattractive, peppery, and difficult to relate to. She apparently had an inner conviction and the stamina to maintain herself in a harsh world which gave her no quarter. She learned to deal with it on her own terms and retained a kind of integrity and honesty and confidence in herself which was revealed in our contacts with her.

On our measures of personality she was consistently well below the mean for the women. Her Reputation Rating was the most negative of all who had been mentioned in the community survey. The panelists for the Community Rating ranked her well below average, in fact near the bottom of the Q-subjects. Three of eight possible Longitudinal Trend Scores for her indicated considerable positive change, and the others indicated little or no change over the years; two Longitudinal Trend Scores could not be obtained because of missing data.

Decliner

Mrs. W.

We found Mrs. W. at age 65 in 1956 still gainfully employed part-time in the drugstore owned by her son. At that time she was married but separated from her husband, and was living alone in her own apartment. She was the mother of two children by an earlier marriage. In 1962, when we next saw her, the husband from whom she had been separated had died and Mrs. W. continued living alone in the same apartment as before. As a young person she had completed the eighth grade, and she had at one time worked as an assistant cook in an orphanage.

At the first two assessment periods Mrs. W. described her health as good, although she felt her serious problems were her "general nervous condition" and heart palpitations, as well as such difficulties as belching, headaches, and constipation. She also mentioned that she had had a nervous breakdown. In 1965 Mrs. W. rated her health as "fair"—although she had spent no days in bed during the year, she was concerned about cataracts as well as the physical problems of the other years.

Mrs. W. maintained membership in a local church, a fire company auxiliary, and a church club, but she did not attend meetings. In 1956, while her activities centered mainly around home, TV, radio, and shopping, she also told us that she spent some time visiting and entertaining. Gradually, however, we found that she concentrated most of her energies upon maintaining her apartment and watching TV. (Her Activity Score declined from 35 to 17 over the nine-year period.) Satisfactions with her activities declined as well, as shown by Attitude Inventory scores of 44 in 1956 and 32 in 1965.

Although Mrs. W. gave few details of her marital problems, she seemed to express bitterness in 1956 concerning her second marriage and the subsequent separation. In our contacts with her she seemed to continue in her low state of morale; in our last contact she tended to feel that her life had been one long series of misfortunes with which she had been almost powerless to deal. In addition to her miserable second marriage, Mrs. W. had experienced the death of her daughter in 1963. She further mentioned her dissatisfaction and resentment toward her meager financial resources. In effect, she felt compelled to ask, "Why me?"

Interviewers reported that Mrs. W. was always neat and clean and that she maintained her old and run-down apartment as well as she could. Over the years she was described as reasonably cooperative and willing to participate in the interview situation after the interviewer succeeded in allaying her initial suspicions.

Our psychometric data showed that, for the initial assessment, Mrs. W.'s scores were all above the means for women at those years, but that scores for subsequent years were generally lower than previously and less than the mean for the group. All except one Longitudinal Trend Score reflected these changes, which were markedly negative, showing decline; the Opinion Conformity score had fluctuated up and then down, and hence the Longitudinal Trend Score was near zero. On the WAIS Similarities, Mrs. W. had an age-scaled score of 6—somewhat below the mean of 7.96.

Mrs. W. was not mentioned either positively or negatively on the 1956 Reputation Rating, nor did she qualify for the Community Rating.

Decliner

Mrs. R.

Mrs. R. was one of the older participants in the study. We first interviewed her in 1956 when she was 76 years old, had been recently widowed, and was living with her daughter and grandson in their home. At age 17 Mrs. R. had left an ungraded school and had worked gainfully for others, doing farm and housework. She and her husband had lived on a farm and had reared five children. At her husband's death, the farm had been sold and Mrs. R. had made the move to her daughter's.

Over the nine-year period of our contacts with Mrs. R., she reported no days spent in bed, although she rated her health mostly as only "fair." Her list of physical problems increased from 1956 to 1965, when she mentioned poor sight and hearing, general rheumatic stiffness, high blood pressure, shortness of breath, swelling of feet, tiredness, aching joints, gas pains, and difficulty in urination. On several occasions she responded to our inquiry about any disadvantages she felt about being her present age as "only not being able to get around physically as well as others can."

During the time we knew her, Mrs. R. moved from the position of having only a few free hours a day (in 1956) to having a half-day free, and (in 1965) to having all day free. Her activities were centered about the house, the yard, and the garden, and did include some visiting and entertaining. Mrs. R. belonged to a Golden Age Club and a church group, but she attended less often now than formerly because of physical limitations and because her daughter, who worked outside the home, was unable to help her get to the meetings. In our last interview, when she was 85, Mrs. R. said that indeed she did a lot of "just sitting and thinking." She stayed in the house alone all day while her grandson and daughter were away, and the interviewer noted in one comment that Mrs. R. really enjoyed the social contact of being interviewed.

While increasing physical problems and social isolation seem to be a part of Mrs. R.'s general lack of social participation, it should be remembered that she had always had a relatively limited social life and that her present state was not new for her nor one which seemed to bother her consciously. She had understood and accepted loneliness for many years. Indeed, to the interviewers who talked with her, she seemed well-adjusted, even accepting the death of her husband in a positive fashion. Her apparent disengagement seemed to have been the result of her circumstances, skills, and health. She saw having her daughter and grandson living with her as an advantage she had over others her age.

In terms of our measures, the pattern is irregular over the years. In some instances her scores were above the mean, just about the mean, or below the mean. On the Activity Inventory there was decline—from 39 to 34 to 24; the Longitudinal Trend Score for this measure was about −.90. Similar decline occurred on the Judge's Rating, the Opinion Conformity Scale, the Interviewer's Rating, and Community Rating. On the P and S there was really no change. On the TAT no Longitudinal Trend Score was available because of missing data.

On the Reputation Rating, Mrs. R. was rated positively; on the Community Rating she was below the mean at all three points in time. On the WAIS Similarities Scale her age-scaled score was 7, while the mean for our longitudinal women was 7.96.

Interpretive Statement Concerning Case Studies

As we examined individuals over the years as presented in the case studies, two generalizations seemed to emerge:

1. Though *change* must necessarily be viewed as relative, *both* change and continuity of personality and adjustment existed in the adults we studied.

2. Though constitutional, group-membership, role, and situational factors undoubtedly influenced the patterns of adjustment of individuals, their influence with our older persons appeared to be *indirect* and not *uni*-directional. We hypothesize the existence in these adults of the mediating influences of a self which enabled them to perceive and interpret and evaluate concrete facts and events and circumstances in ways that made them acceptable to those individuals even as they were measured by our instruments as "decliners," "improvers," or "maintainers."

For example, although physical health would surely be an influence upon adjustment in the later years, we found good health to be associated with both decline and improvement. Conversely, we saw persons who, objectively speaking, possessed rather severe physical impairments, but who nevertheless improved or maintained their personality and adjustment pattern over time. Chronological age itself did not appear to be a direct influence upon either positive or negative change.

Nor did economic security, ample educational background, or religious affiliation *per se* appear to guarantee positive change. Improver-maintainers were found among persons who had strong group memberships and many intimate contacts, as well as among persons who, to outside evaluators at least, seemed to have few such contacts. Indeed, some of the persons who were classified as improvers were not well known and not visible to other persons in the community in terms of their being mentioned one way or another in our study of reputations. In addition, some individuals who were classified in the improver-maintainer category did not seem especially pleasant or attractive to others. Miss C., for example, was seen as a bitter, peppery, physically unattractive old maid, yet she appeared to possess a dogged, personal integrity that enabled her to sustain herself and interpret her own situation in a satisfactory, self-maintaining fashion.

It might also be asked whether whole series or combinations of factors contributed to change positively or negatively. We do not feel that the answer to this question would provide an adequate explanation. We would propose rather that, among adults at least, with their capacity to evaluate, remember, sum up, hypothesize, and integrate experience, highly specific events and influences are less potent uni-directional influences. The older person becomes less of a passive responder and more of an active perceiver and mediator than he was formerly.

SUMMARY

In this chapter we posed questions of central concern: How do personality and adjustment change over the latter part of the life span? What personal and social factors are related to such continuity and change? We discussed some matters of research design, and then, dealt with the concepts under scrutiny. Criteria for selecting techniques of measurements were set down, and then each measure was explained in detail.

In presenting the findings, we described the longitudinal study group in terms of background information and of their performance on measures of personality and adjustment. In addition, individual change was observed through use of longitudinal trend scores. Attempts to issolate factors related to change or stability were made through statistical analyses and through analyses of several individual case studies.

Chapter 4

Aging and Survival

To age is to continue living, to survive, and in his most basic activities man's goal is to live. Lorus and Margery Milne have put it this way:

> Surely no purpose outranks survival. All other purposes are secondary. . . . No single pattern ensures survival. . . (and) no single feature provides the answer. . . . Through the complexities of life shine the patterns that have meant survival. Hidden in the rocks, in the bodies and ways of life of plants and animals is the mindless wisdom of at least 2 billion years. With his superb brain, man is ready to learn from nonhuman inhabitants of his solar system and perhaps more distant worlds. He can seek to discover how his own kind and other creatures have survived so far, while so many have disappeared without issue. By finding and applying the pattern of survival, man is most likely to extend his own future" (Milne and Milne, 1967, pp. xi-xii).

THE QUESTIONS

When we *experienced* the rapid attrition of our study population and contemplated its meaning, we were convinced we had to try to replace our wonderment with answers to our second basic question of how survival is related to personality and adjustment. That survival is in the *last* analysis a biological process is clear, we thought. In a "semi-final" analysis, however, what social and psychological characteristics are related to survival? Do any such variables differentiate survivors from nonsurvivors? In these dimensions, how *selective* is the aging and survival process? How well does a surviving population of older adults represent the total group of which it was once a part? And how is *change* in the social and psychological character we were studying related to survival?

These are the central questions of this chapter. Our thinking was that women would outlive men and that younger subjects would outlive older ones, naturally. Further, we hypothesized that those individuals who were actively involved in the social system and who lived under economic and social conditions which promoted such involvement would survive those who did not, and that those who received satisfaction from their active participation and felt well about themselves in the process would also survive. Still further, we thought that those persons who over the years *continued* patterns of satisfying involvement would survive those who, for one reason or another, did not continue such patterns.

This reasoning suggests that continuing activity and "engagement" are optimal for survival—in contrast to becoming progressively inactive and withdrawn or "disengaged" (Cumming and Henry, 1961), whether initiated by one's physiology, by one's psychological being, and/or by social forces. This rests upon the conception that, like all normally functioning men and women, older people, functioning normally, fundamentally want to continue *living* in the best possible manner. Continuing to live means continuing to be actively involved in their own uniquely meaningful patterns, rather than moving to prepare themselves progressively to die—death being the ultimate form of disengagement. In these ways man, unlike lower animals, continues until death to control in part the quality of his life and to be at least partially responsible for his own survival.

These hypotheses are exaggerations of our expectations, since we basically cannot discard the fact that failure of the biological organism to continue its basic functions is the fundamental cause of death. These statements illustrate, however, the nature of our search for factors that may, as we have said, be associated in some "semi-final" way with biological functioning.

To answer our questions we needed information on *all* the subjects individually listed in our initial rounds. Comparison could then be made of survivors and nonsurvivors at various points later in time. Obviously, a longitudinal design was required.

SOME RELATED RESEARCH

In computing its life expectancy tables, the United States Public Health Service presents death rates according to sex, age, race, and location of residence. For a white male aged 65 in the United States the average remaining years of life in 1967 was 13.0 years; for a white female it was 16.5 years (U.S. Bureau of the

Census, 1969, p. 53). In 1959-1961, the expectancy was 12.97 and 15.88 years, respectively (U.S. Bureau of the Census, 1969, p. 53). For Pennsylvanians in the same categories, average expected life was 12.32 years for males and 14.96 years for females (Brotman, 1967, p. 12).

Analyses by the Metropolitan Life Insurance Company have shown variations in death rates according to socioeconomic variables (Metropolitan Life Insurance Company, 1967; 1968a; 1968b; 1968c). The work of Kitagawa and Hauser, in which 340,000 Americans were studied, emphasizes the important contribution of "socioeconomic epidemiology":

> It is of great significance that mortality from most of the causes of death varies considerably with socioeconomic status as measured by educational attainment. . . . The possibility of reducing mortality through improved control of social and economic conditions assumes an especially great significance in the light of the relatively static state of not only the general death rate but the age-specific death rates in the United States since about 1950 (Kitagawa and Hauser, 1968, p. 349).

The positive associations of educational level to survival rates, as shown by much earlier studies of mortality, particularly of infants and mothers, was examined in relation to eugenics by Osborn in *The Future of Human Heredity* (1968).

Other research points to the role nonbiomedical factors and *change* in such variables may have in death or survival: the Duke Longitudinal Study (Palmore, 1970); the longitudinal studies of twins and their intelligence made by Jarvik and her associates (1962, 1963, 1967); the studies of cognitive and personality change of Riegel and his colleagues (Riegel, Riegel, and Meyer, 1967a, 1967b; Riegel and Riegel, 1970); the research on intellectual functioning by Kleemeier (1961, 1962); Kleemeier, Justiss, Rich and Jones (1961), Sanderson and Inglis (1961), Berkowitz (1965), Reimanis and Green (1971), and Baltes, Schaie, and Nardi (1971); and investigations of sensory decline (Beard, 1969) and of personality functioning (Butler, 1963, 1967; Lieberman, 1965, 1966, 1969). In addition, questions of the impact of retirement (McMahan and Ford, 1955; Thompson, 1958), of relocation (Bloom, Blenkner, and Markus, 1969;

Increase in Death Rates, 1969; Lieberman, 1961; Lieberman and Lakin, 1963), and of widowhood (Kraus and Lilienfeld, 1959; Berardo, 1970) have received attention. All point to the conclusion that social and psychological variables do seem to function importantly in processes of survival or nonsurvival. Our investigation was designed to provide some understanding of these functions.

THE METHOD

The house-to-house survey in the summer of 1955 provided us with a listing of all residents of the village of Pennsboro and the surrounding Centre township. In 1950 the population of this geographical area totaled almost 2,000; in 1960 there were some 75 fewer persons (U.S. Bureau of the Census, 1961). In 1955 we listed 205 who were then aged *64* or over. These numbers were determined by calling at each living unit in the study area and listing the occupants' names, ages, occupations, etc. The following summer, when we were ready to proceed with our more intensive study of older adults, we called at the home of each person then 65 or over for the purpose of interviewing him or her. At that time we located 176 persons, as we have explained previously.

We repeated the process in 1962 and again in 1965, locating our subjects when we could and interviewing them with our follow-up procedures. Frequently, family members or neighbors explained what had happened to them if they no longer lived where they did. We regularly verified such statements with other community members who knew the facts.

By such processes we were able to derive successive lists of eligible subjects by "disposing" of those who had moved away or died. We then could proceed, and eventually we classified all eligible subjects in one of these categories: too ill (or old) to be interviewed, refused to be interviewed, or interviewed. The last included those from whom we had obtained more or less complete information, or even "abbreviated" information through use of a shortened, abstract schedule. The latter was used when it was clear to the interviewer that the subject could not complete the interview because of his mental and/or physical condition or his reluctance to participate. Outright refusals were accepted only after at least one repeated call, usually by another interviewer. The categories of "moved" or "too ill" were used only when verified by community informants or actual observation of the eligible subject. We did learn that most of those who moved did so because of these reasons: they sought hospital or nursing home care, of which none was available in the study area; or they were no longer able to maintain themselves in their current living arrangements and had moved to be near their children or others who could help sustain them.

At later points in time we updated our lists of subjects to continue our study of survival. This we did in 1967, in 1969, and again in 1971. This process included keeping track of subjects' deaths as reported in the local weekly newspaper and then going over our lists again with consultants in the community.

ANALYSIS

Characteristics of our subjects, as described by the survey of 1955, formed the baseline data for comparing successive waves of surviving and nonsurviving men and women. For the subjects interviewed in 1956, additional comparisons could be made, using demographic and other information, including our measures of personality and adjustment. These comparisons were made by means of chi-square tests to determine the statistical significance of differences between survivors and nonsurvivors. We also attempted to describe those who refused our queries in an effort to understand problems of older persons' participation in community-based research. Let us turn to these findings.

THE FINDINGS

Attrition of the Subjects over the Years

The "census" taken in 1955 of the study area, including the village and the surrounding township, listed 205 persons aged 64 or older—80 men and 125 women. These numbers were the bases for our successive analyses of survivorship (see Tables 20 to 23). When classified in 1956, when all subjects were then aged 65 or over, only 68 of the original 80 men and 108 of the original 125 women (a total of 176 of the 205 persons) remained. Twelve, mostly women, had moved away, but 17 had died within that one year. Thus 176 persons, or 86 percent, were eligible for our first (longitudinal) interviewing in 1956; the remaining 14 percent had died or moved out of the study area. And of the 176 eligible subjects, we interviewed 146, or 83 percent (Table 20).

TABLE 20

Classification of 1955 Subjects in *1956*

	Men		Women		Total	
1956 Category	N	%	N	%	N	%
Total *1955* age 64+ population	80	101	125	100	205	100
Moved away	2	3	10	8	12	6
Died	10	13	7	6	17	8
Living and in area	68	85	108	86	176	86
Total eligible Ss, *1956*	68	100	108	101	176	101
Too ill	2	3	6	6	8	5
Refused	7	10	15	14	22	13
Interviewed	59	87	87	81	146	83

What happened over the years to our study population? Tables 21 to 23 provide this information for 1962, 1965, 1967, 1969, and 1971. In 1962, 46 percent of the original 205—31 men and 64 women—were still living and in the area, and 85 percent of these were interviewed and tested (Table 21). By 1965, at the time of our third wave of interviewing the older residents, only 34 percent of the original group were still living and available—24 men and 46 women. Fifty-three persons, 19 men and 34 women, were interviewed at this point in the study (Table 22).

To carry our analyses of survivorship further into time, we updated our lists of subjects with the help of the obituary columns in the local newspaper and of consultants in the community. This we did in 1967, when all our subjects would have been at least 76 years of age, again in 1969, and again in 1971, when all would have been 80 years or older. These data are shown in Table 23.

By 1967 almost three-fourths of the originally eligible men had died, a few had moved away, and about one-fifth were still living and in the area. Over one-half (55 percent) of the women

TABLE 21

Classification of 1955 Subjects in *1962*

1962 Category	Men		Women		Total	
	N	%	N	%	N	%
Total *1955* age 64+ population	80	100	125	100	205	100
Moved away	5	6	15	12	20	10
Died	44	55	46	37	90	44
Living and in area	31	39	64	51	95	46
Total eligible Ss, *1962*	31	100	64	100	95	100
Too ill	2	6	3	5	5	5
Refused	3	10	6	9	9	10
Interviewed	26	84	55	86	81[a]	85

[a]Of these, 71 persons (24 men and 47 women) were interviewed in both 1956 and 1962.

TABLE 22

Classification of 1955 Subjects in *1965*

1965 Category	Men		Women		Total	
	N	%	N	%	N	%
Total *1955* age 64+ population	80	100	125	100	205	100
Moved away	3	4	16	13	19	9
Died	53	66	63	50	116	57
Living and in area	24	30	46	37	70	34
Total eligible Ss, *1965*	24	100	46	101	70	100
Too ill	—	—	3	7	3	4
Refused	5	21	9	20	14	20
Interviewed	19	79	34	74	53[a]	76

[a]Of these, 46 persons (17 men and 29 women) were interviewed in 1956 and 1962 and 1965. These are the "longitudinal subjects."

had died, one-eighth had moved, and about one-third, 40, were still living in the area. Thus, in 1967, a total of 58 (28 percent) of the original 205 subjects were still living and in the area. Two years later, in 1969, the data show additional attrition in our population: two-thirds of our subjects had died, and only 22

TABLE 23

Classification of 1955 Subjects in 1967, 1969, and 1971

Category	Men		Women		Total	
	N	%	N	%	N	%
1967						
Total 1955 age 64+ population	80	101	125	100	205	99
Moved away	3	4	16	13	19	9
Died	59	74	69	55	128	62
Living and in area	18	23	40	32	58	28
1969						
Total 1955 age 64+ population	80	100	125	100	205	100
Moved away	5	6	17	14	22	11
Died	60	75	78	62	138	67
Living and in area	15	19	30	24	45	22
1971						
Total 1955 age 64+ population	80	100	125	100	205	100
Moved away	5	6	14	11	19	9
Died	67	84	93	74	160	78
Living and in area	8	10	18	14	26	13

percent remained alive and in the study area. By 1971, over three-quarters (78 percent) had died, 9 percent had moved away, and only 13 percent were still living in the community. Proportionally more women were living, but the difference in proportions decreases.

Thus, in a sixteen-year period—somewhat less than a generation—from 1955 to 1971, only 8 out of 80 men and 18 out of 125 women were still living and eligible to participate if we had followed them up again. We did not, for several reasons, chief of which was that many of our subjects had found it so taxing physically and emotionally in our last round of interviewing in 1965 that we felt we could not pursue them further on a direct basis.

Comparisons of Survivors and Nonsurvivors

How different were our survivors from those who did not survive? How well did our survivors represent the original subject population? The importance of this question to the study of development and change over time has been underscored by Riegel, Riegel, and Meyer (1967b), when they said:

> Development as reflected by trends. . . would be a meaningful concept only if the dropout of subjects in consecutive age groups is strictly a random process. . . . Age samples drawn from cross-sectional studies or followed up in longitudinal studies become increasingly biased, the further one moves upward in the age scale, and thus the generalized trend will be confounded by the increasing degree of sample bias (Riegel, Riegel, and Meyer, 1967b, p. 347).

Survey Data

To explore the question of bias by survival, we used our baseline survey data of 1955 to compare survivors and nonsurvivors among the total eligible study population that year. These results for successive waves of follow-up tabulations are shown in Table 24, in the form of chi-square values for the various factors. *Survival is defined as living and in the area* rather than simply living; this probably has more import for women than for men, since more women than men moved from the area and, so far as we could determine, were still living but no longer in the community (Tables 20 to 23). Note that certain comparisons could not be made because expected frequencies were insufficiently large.

First, chi-square comparisons were made between men and women according to survivorship. As shown by the table footnote, women significantly outlived men in our 1962 analysis, but not in the analyses of 1956, 1965, 1967, 1969, or 1971. It appears that after a certain point sex differences were not so important. Age was a factor differentiating surviving and nonsurviving women at three points in the analysis, and at four points in time for men. There were fewer deaths among younger subjects than among older ones.

Marital status and living arrangements (with whom are you living?) in 1955 did not, at any point in the analysis, differentiate survivors from those who died. Education made no difference, either, except in the 1962 and 1969 analyses for men, when the

TABLE 24

Chi-Square Values for Factors Comparing Survivors[a] and Nonsurvivors[a] Among Total Original 1955 Study Population Aged 64 and Over, by Sex and Year of Comparison

Factor	Men[b]						Women[b]					
	1956	1962	1965	1967	1969	1971	1956	1962	1965	1967	1969	1971
Age	4.50*	7.65*	8.03*	3.40	1.62	4.52*	#	8.90*	9.90*	7.39*	3.51	.24
Marital status	.43	1.98	2.78	3.01	3.07	2.54	#	.03	.06	.26	.83	.40
Living arrangements	1.96	2.07	2.85	3.19	3.13	2.59	#	.19	.95	.13	.63	.30
Education	1.71	3.89*	1.98	3.17	4.30*	.02	#	2.48	.88	1.04	.03	1.65
Occupation of family wage earner	#	7.92*	6.58*	.80	.45	#	#	21.58*	9.47*	7.24*	4.10	3.81
Residence—borough vs. outside borough	.06	.74	.74	.15	1.39	.02	#	.77	.76	10.80*	9.97	.71

[a]Survivors are defined as those verified as living *and* in the study area; nonsurvivors are those known to have died.

[b]Women significantly often outlived men in 1962 (x^2 = 5.20*), not in 1956 (x^2 = 2.71), not in 1965 (x^2 = 2.34), not in 1967 (x^2 = 3.79), not in 1969 (x^2 = 1.44), and not in 1971 (x^2 = 1.15).

*Significant at the 5 or less than 5 percent level; df = 1, except for occupation of family wage earner, when df = 2.

#Expected frequencies too small for calculation of chi-square.

better educated men tended to outlive less well-educated men. Place of residence—the village or outside its limits—was related only to women's survival and then only in 1967, when those within the borough survived more frequently than those outside.

The factor of occupation of the family wage earner was most consistently related to survival at the earlier points of assessment, when survivors tended significantly to come from families whose wage earner was of a higher status occupation.

Interview Data

In Table 25, chi-square data comparing surviving and nonsurviving *interviewees* of 1956 are presented. Sex was not a differentiating factor in any of the years of analysis. Age significantly differentiated surviving and nonsurviving women at three early points, when younger women outlived the older ones in the study; age did not differentiate surviving men. Marital status, living arrangements, education, and employment status (working full-time or part-time versus not working) were generally not differentiating factors. Higher occupational status was related to survival at certain points but not at others.

Women who in 1956 rated their health as fair or poor or very poor tended not to survive the years that followed; women who rated their health as good or excellent survived significantly more often. Apparently there is validity to their ratings of health, but not to men's; women who rated their health as good or excellent in 1956 tended to outlive other women who considered themselves in poor health at all points in the analysis.

Table 26 presents chi-square results of comparisons, using our measures of personality and adjustment. Again, the analysis used the 1956 baseline data, conceived of as antecedent variables. None of the measures distinguished surviving men from nonsurviving men. Apparently scores on the measures in 1956 were not predictive of death in later years for men.

The women, however, with higher scores on the Activity Inventory, the Attitude Inventory, and the Judge's Rating, tended significantly often to outlive those with lower scores on the measures. These three measures are laden with a strong activity dimension (Britton, 1962). According to our measurements, the more active women tended to outlive the less active ones, but active men did not survive more frequently than inactive men.

TABLE 25

Chi-Square Values for Factors Comparing Survivors[a] and Nonsurvivors[a] Among 1956 *Interviewees* by Sex and Year of Comparison

Factor	Men[b]					Women[b]				
	1962	1965	1967	1969	1971	1962	1965	1967	1969	1971
Age	1.78	3.02	.89	.12	1.86	9.67*	10.06*	9.44*	3.43	.85
Marital status	1.42	.69	1.46	1.43	1.02	.02	.01	1.63	3.68	1.91
Living arrangements	1.51	.91	1.46	1.43	1.02	.01	.06	1.16	3.13	1.60
Education	3.49	1.94	2.30	5.53*	.06	2.38	1.70	1.57	.01	1.41
Occupation of family wage earner	5.48*	3.28	.19	.21	1.88	16.74*	3.19	5.07*	2.17	1.73
Employment status	.32	.15	1.03	.64	.75	.29	.31	1.47	.50	.42
Health status	.42	.03	.01	.21	1.28	8.49*	13.93*	12.10*	10.57*	5.96*

[a]Survivors are defined as those verified as living *and* in the study area; nonsurvivors are those known to have died.
[b]Men and women interviewees did not differ significantly from each other on survival in 1962 (χ^2 = 2.73), 1965 (χ^2 = 1.01), 1967 (χ^2 = 2.35), 1969 (χ^2 = .76), or in 1971 (χ^2 = 2.32).
*Significant at the 5 or less than 5 percent level; df = 1.

TABLE 26

Chi-Square Values for Measures of Personality and Adjustment Comparing Survivors[a] and Nonsurvivors[a] Among 1956 Interviewees by Sex and Year of Comparison

Factor	Men[b]					Women[b]				
	1962	1965	1967	1969	1971	1962	1965	1967	1969	1971
Activity Inventory	1.43	1.18	.01	.08	#	3.56	6.57*	7.58*	5.48*	3.17
Attitude Inventory	.70	1.40	1.43	3.35	#	6.57*	9.07*	8.50*	7.46*	4.59*
Judge's Rating	1.26	.98	.58	2.53	#	11.40*	12.12*	10.70*	5.74*	6.56*
Personal Relations and Sociability Scale	.15	.07	.88	2.24	#	1.10	1.58	1.84	2.48	1.93
Thematic Apperception Test	.60	.65	.28	1.17	#	.89	.01	.75	.17	.77
Opinion Conformity Scale	.08	1.37	.19	.02	#	4.53*	.12	.01	.00	.02
Interviewer's Rating	.54	2.35	3.52	2.51	#	3.02	.52	3.25	4.45*	1.64
Reputation Rating	2.44	2.42	.20	.90	#	.01	.02	.00	.00	.26

[a] Survivors are defined as those verified as living *and* in the study area; nonsurvivors are those known to have died.
[b] Men and women interviewees did not differ significantly on survivorship in 1962, 1965, 1967, 1969, or in 1971 (see Table 25).
*Significant at the 5 or less than 5 percent level; $df = 1$.
Expected frequencies too small for calculation of chi-square.

Scores on the other measures—the TAT, the Opinion Conformity Scale (except 1962), the Personal Relations and Sociability Scale, the Interviewer's Rating (except 1969), and the Reputation Rating—did not differentiate the survivors from nonsurvivors.

In sum, our analysis showed few social or psychological factors associated with death or survival. Age seemed to be a factor of survival for women more than for men, particularly when interviewees (a somewhat selective group) are compared. Social status, measured crudely by the occupational status of the family wage earner, seemed to be an important consideration, but more so for women than for men. We might hypothesize somewhat differing life styles for women of high social status, a point hypothetically corroborated by the relevancy for survival of our activity-laden measures of personality and adjustment. For men there were apparently no factors relevant to life style that consistently differentiated survivors. We are led to believe, then, that other factors, probably genetic or biological ones, hold greater power over the male members than over the female members of the species. It is possible, even likely, that females are taught and learn to monitor and regulate, consciously and/or unconsciously, the functioning of their bodies. Men, on the other hand, may learn to deny, disregard, or conceal, especially from themselves, signs of illness or malfunction in their bodies. Their lack of awareness might result in less perceptiveness about their health and to less use of preventive measures or ameliorative intervention.

Change in Measures of Personality and Adjustment

Analysis of data concerning *change* over the years of the study failed to show factors consistently related to survival. Information on change in our measures of personality and adjustment over time might, we thought, shed some light on the problem of the nature of surviving adults. This follows the lead of other investigators who have studied the antecedents of death and have shown "anticipatory" changes in intellectual and personality functioning (Kleemeier, 1961, 1962; Riegel, Riegel, and Meyer, 1967a, 1967b; Lieberman, 1965). The problem was to determine whether or not *change* in any of our measures from 1956 to 1965 was predictive of death or survival in 1967, in 1969, or in 1971, our later points of reference. Here we used our *longitudinal subjects* (see Chapter 2) and the measures of continuity or change from 1956 to 1965, the Longitudinal Trend Scores (LTS's; see Chapter 3).

Let us first determine the disposition of our *longitudinal* subjects over the years following their last assessment in 1965. These data are shown in Table 27. In 1967, two years after the final collection of data from these subjects, 12 of the 17 men and 24 of the 29 women were still living and residing in the area—71 percent and 83 percent, respectively. More men than women had died and a few had moved away. (As we said earlier, moving out of the community often was for the purpose of obtaining extended care and often preceded death.) After another two years, an additional man and two additional women had died, and a few had moved away—leaving 59 percent and 66 percent of the men and women, respectively, living and residing in the area. By July 1971,

TABLE 27

Classification of Longitudinal Subjects in 1967, 1969, and 1971

Category	Men		Women		Total	
	N	%	N	%	N	%
1967						
Total Longitudinal Ss	17	100	29	100	46	100
Moved away	1	6	2	7	3	7
Died	4	23	3	10	7	15
Living and in area	12	71	24	83	36	78
1969						
Total Longitudinal Ss	17	100	29	100	46	100
Moved away	2	12	5	17	7	15
Died	5	29	5	17	10	22
Living and in area	10	59	19	66	29	63
1971						
Total Longitudinal Ss	17	100	29	100	46	100
Moved away	2	12	5	17	7	15
Died	11	65	13	45	24	52
Living and in area	4	23	11	38	15	33

several more of the longitudinal subjects had died, and only 23 percent of the men and 38 percent of the women were still living and making their homes in the area.

In an effort to increase our understanding about behavioral change in relation to survival, we have attempted to present data (Table 28) that might show the extent to which survivors and nonsurvivors differed on the LTS's. The data should be viewed cautiously since numbers are small in the survival categories; moreover, N's vary considerably on the Longitudinal Trend Scores. The figures for the LTS's are means of the *coded* LTS's, using a code for the analytical procedures that eliminated positive and negative LTS's. The code ranged from 01 (which stood for LTS's from −.90 to −1.00) to 09 (−.01 to −.10) for those with a negative direction, and from 10 (standing for the LTS's ranging from +.01 to +.10) to 20 (+.90 to +1.00) for the LTS's with a positive direction.

In addition to LTS data, scores on the Similarities Scale of the Wechsler Adult Intelligence Scale (Wechsler, 1955), administered in 1965, were included. Comparisons are between those longitudinal subjects who died and those who continued living to three points in time −1967, 1969, and 1971.

The hypothesis was that those who died had changed for the worse more often than those who continued to live; operationally this meant that the coded averages for the LTS's should be lower for the subjects who died than for those who continued to live. The results show that where there were differences in the LTS's in the predicted direction, the differences were slight at all three points in the analysis. Often the direction of the differences was in the reverse of that predicted, but numbers were indeed small. This was true for both men and women. Our hypothesis does not appear to be confirmed. (See also the discussion of Botwinick, 1967.)

When comparing the living versus the dead on the WAIS Similarities Test, both raw and age-scaled scores, there were no consistent or marked differences. Scores on this test of intellectual functioning were not apparently predictive of survival or death.

SUMMARY

The questions for this portion of our study concerned the social-psychological correlates of survival. We asked how different

TABLE 28

Means of Longitudinal Trend Scores (Coded) and of WAIS Scores (1965)
for Longitudinal Ss, According to Sex and Survival Classification
in 1967, 1969, and 1971

	Men		Women	
Classification and Measure	Died	Living	Died	Living
Eligible Ss in 1965 (N)	—	(17)	—	(29)
LTS x 1967 Classification (N)	(4)	(12)	(3)	(24)
Activity Inventory	8.7	6.3	18.0	6.9
Attitude Inventory	10.3	5.6	10.0	8.1
Judge's Rating	8.7	8.3	10.0	6.9
Personal Relations and Sociability Scale	13.0	7.8	8.7	9.5
Thematic Apperception Test	18.0	14.8	9.5	11.5
Opinion Conformity Scale	8.5	10.3	8.0	8.3
Interviewer's Rating	11.0	5.5	7.3	2.4
Community Rating (Q)	1.0	20.0	—	4.6
(WAIS Similarities, Raw Score)	20.7	17.3	13.7	14.5
(WAIS Similarities, Age-Scaled Score)	21.7	17.8	16.0	17.7
LTS x 1969 Classification (N)	(5)	(10)	(5)	(19)
Activity Inventory	8.2	6.5	12.2	7.7
Attitude Inventory	8.0	6.7	5.5	8.5
Judge's Rating	7.0	8.2	7.6	7.8
Personal Relations and Sociability Scale	11.0	8.6	12.0	9.5
Thematic Apperception Test	17.7	14.9	10.7	10.8
Opinion Conformity Scale	9.3	11.2	5.2	9.7
Interviewer's Rating	8.5	6.1	5.4	2.2
Community Rating (Q)	1.0	20.0	—	6.0
(WAIS Similarities, Raw Score)	19.7	17.3	15.4	14.3
(WAIS Similarities, Age-Scaled Score)	21.3	19.8	17.8	17.4
LTS x 1971 Classification (N)	(10)	(4)	(12)	(12)
Activity Inventory	8.3	1.8	8.3	8.4
Attitude Inventory	7.4	2.7	5.1	9.7
Judge's Rating	9.3	4.0	6.7	7.3
Personal Relations and Sociability Scale	9.4	7.8	11.0	9.7
Thematic Apperception Test	14.8	17.3	11.5	10.0
Opinion Conformity Scale	12.0	7.3	8.3	7.0
Interviewer's Rating	7.6	5.8	3.2	3.1
Community Rating (Q)	10.5	20.0	2.5	4.8
(WAIS Similarities, Raw Score)	17.5	15.0	15.4	16.0
(WAIS Similarities, Age-Scaled Score)	20.0	18.5	17.7	19.1

survivors were from nonsurvivors among our subjects, using demographic and psychological data available on the total original subject population and additional information on our longitudinal subjects. In the analysis, we traced the gradual attrition of the original subjects over sixteen years—from the total of 205 enumerated in 1955 to 26 listed in 1971 as living and residing in the area; only 15 of the 46 longitudinal subjects were living and located in the study community in 1971.

The analysis showed few, if any, social and psychological variables, including sex, that were consistently related to survival among our subjects. Sex-related factors, such as apparently differing perceptions of health and illness, and also occupational status, suggested diverse life styles which themselves might be associated with survival. Data on change in our measures of personality and adjustment showed no measure predictive of survivorship.

Chapter 5

The Place of the Old
in a Small Community

A small town, say those from the land of the concrete canyons, is Squaresville, U.S.A.; the kind of place, man, where the cats really do go "meow" and where the only swingers are old women swaying to and fro on the front porch.

The slickers don't stop there. A small town, they sneer, is Hick Heaven where only three things happen—morning, noon and night; where everybody knows everybody else's business; where gossip is the leading civic pastime, and where a hot spot is a bench on the sunny side of the courthouse yard.

On the other hand, a small town has certain distinctions (actually virtues) that never are seen by the demeanors who pass through maybe once or twice and become instant, all-inclusive experts.

For a small town also is a place where there are more trees than people; where the city slickers go to get outsmarted; where you don't have to count your change; where birthdays are remembered and business is done on a first-name basis; where people go home to lunch, and where the barbershop is the only place you can get clipped.

What is more, a small town is a place you leave in order to make enough money to return to live.

—*"Joe Creason's Kentucky"* (1969)

To understand the patterns of adjustment of any person, it is useful to know the position he occupies in the social structure and to recognize the special ways of believing and behaving which his social group holds. Since different segments of society may have different behavioral expectations for persons in varying age, sex, and social categories, it is of value to define these expectations and to determine the manner in which individuals respond to them.

For purposes of the present study, adjustment was defined so as to include not only "inner" (or "covert") behavior but also "outer" (or "social") behavior. The unity of these two areas is expressed by the idea that an individual must be able to satisfy his own needs by behaving in accordance with society's expectations. Cavan, Burgess, Havighurst, and Goldhamer have stated this view:

> Personal adjustment . . . may be defined as the individual's restructuring of his attitudes and behavior in response to a new situation in such a way as to integrate the expression of his aspirations with the expectations and demands of society (1949, p. 11).

THE RESEARCH PROBLEM

As part of our research we set out to learn what social norms or expectations residents of Pennsboro and Green Township held for older people. We shall summarize those findings here. They are seen primarily as a "backdrop" or an attitudinal setting for our older subjects, and perhaps as distinctive from actual relationships and behavior within the study community (Harlan, 1964). We also wanted to learn something about the reputations older individuals had in relation to social norms. Because we wished to compare typical psychometric personality assessment procedures with "real-life" assessments, we studied a special sample of our subjects by obtaining appraisals by community members. We shall report these results in this chapter. In addition, we shall discuss some of our impressions of how a small rural community is as a place to live and grow old.

EXPECTATIONS FOR
OLDER MEMBERS OF THE COMMUNITY

Two reviews (Streib and Thompson, 1960; Williams, 1960) have emphasized the importance of social norms in determining the roles, status, and relationships of older adults. As described previously, a first step in our data collection was to conduct a survey of every household in the study community for two purposes: (1) identifying each older person in the community, and (2) learning what expectations adults held regarding older people and their behavior. This effort was intended to help us gain a perspective of the behavioral realities confronting older people in Liberty County. Theoretically, while norms prescribe standard ways of acting and some groups may emphasize conformity to them, norms nevertheless may permit certain latitudes of deviation. As such, norms might well be thought of as *principles* of behavior rather than detailed prescriptions. And because of the variety of groups to which an individual might belong, even within a small community, it would be expected that neither universal norms would exist nor universal conformity would be expected. This would be true of the behaviors involved in the life problems of aging. Such problems are complex and typically involve other persons, including persons of different statuses with different and sometimes conflicting social roles to perform. Thus, norms evolve and change, and this process theoretically enables (often too slowly) individuals and societies to adapt to changing demands and circumstances.

Procedure

The interview schedule (Appendix C) was organized around problems of older persons and ways to cope with them: retirement, living arrangements, family relationships, community participation, and the solution of personal problems. As explained in Chapter 2, two kinds of items were used: open-ended questions and anecdotal questions. Following each anecdote, the interviewer asked the respondent to tell what he thought about the behavior just described. The replies to these relatively unstructured interviewing procedures illustrated how people in the community felt about various problems of aging. The answers were tabulated as they supported different viewpoints; we place emphasis here on the general views about aging, as advocated within the study community. Elsewhere the results have been presented by means of an alternative form of analysis (Britton, Mather, and Lansing, 1961a, 1961b, and 1962; Britton and Britton, 1962).

In connection with the solving of personal problems we queried professional persons who serviced, or whose organizations serviced, the mental health needs of older adults in Liberty County. We also talked individually with organizational leaders about their views of older persons' needs. The intent in both surveys was to determine the extent of attention explicity given to older persons' welfare, broadly defined, and the extent to which professional services were actually used (Britton, 1958). We shall include a brief summary of these findings.

Subjects

The participants in the community-wide, house-to-house canvas numbered 487—102 men and 385 women (see Chapter 2). The *potential* subject population consisted of one adult for each of the 540 households in the community. We succeeded in obtaining normative data from 487, or 90.2 percent of them. The population interviewed was overrepresented by women, which was natural enough since interviewing was done primarily during working hours. The men interviewed tended to be older than the women. Younger respondents tended to have had more schooling than older ones. While these subjects are not really representative of all adults in Pennsboro and Green Township, they gave us information about some of the normative aspects of the community for the behavior of older persons. By virtue of our open-ended, anecdotal inquiry, we cannot and do not generally refer to the norms in a quantitative sense, especially in view of the biases in our participating group. The findings show some of the complexities and qualifications which behavioral situations in several areas of living call forth. After presentation of these findings, we shall discuss the results of our analysis of types of interviewees who emphasized one or another view in the several areas.

Work and Retirement

The interest here pertained to the meaning of work and the significance of retirement, and the factors that determine when a person can and should retire. Open-ended, anecdotal questions stimulated discussion of such matters as financial self-sufficiency, the desirability of retirement as a means of releasing jobs for younger people, and the use of a specific chronological age as a criterion. The results are presented in the interpretive summary which follows.

"When do you think a person should retire?" About half the respondents said that retirement should depend upon a person's health, but approximately the same percentage approved the notion that retirement should occur at a specific age—generally between 60 and 70. By comparison, there was little support for the idea that retirement should depend on individual circumstances, that older people should retire to make jobs available for young people, or that retirement should take place when individuals wanted to take advantage of the good times it could offer for their later years.

Liberty County adults also appeared to hold the opinion that it is important for an older person to keep active (either with his job or with hobbies) as long as his health permits. Nearly half the respondents expressed this idea directly, with lesser proportions emphasizing the value of activity: "It's bad for a man to stop working"; "It's good for a man to work even part-time because it gives him something to do"; and, "A person should never retire; he should always do something."

The participants in the study generally believed that it is all right for a man to retire and turn his business over to his son and stay around to advise the son. However, nearly 40 percent of the adults added the qualification that this would be wise only if father and son can get along. About 20 percent were doubtful that fathers and sons could get along in such a way: "That doesn't usually work out," they said. More adults, about one-third, felt it would be more appropriate for a retired man to help out in the business when things get rushed than to offer advice.

Although attitudes toward job and retirement depended upon the situation with which the respondent was confronted, over half the respondents considered retiring at age 65 and going on public assistance to be a bad thing to do. A number of alternatives to public assistance were offered: "A man should save his money so he won't have to go on public assistance"; "He should get an easier job if he is unable to do the one he has, rather than go on public assistance"; or, "When a couple is almost out of money, they should work harder or spend less."

Living Arrangements and Family Relationships

In the area of living arrangements and family relationships, our adult respondents tended to feel that older persons and their grown children should associate as the two generations themselves see fit. It seemed preferable to the respondents that the two generations not live together. Forty-three percent replied that even a recently widowed woman should stay in her own home or live alone rather than with her children. Similar opinions, though from a smaller proportion of respondents, were offered: "Older people should not live with the family because conflicts are apt to occur," or "Older people should live alone because they are happier being independent."

Almost one-third of the respondents, however, felt that if satisfactory arrangements could be worked out the two generations could live together: "It's all right for a widow and her daughter to live together if they can get along." Other reasons for living together which were condoned included persons' inability to care for themselves, financial difficulties, or loneliness. Nevertheless, when asked about specific circumstances, such as an older woman starting to act "queer" (senile), a man becoming too feeble to care for himself, or a woman no longer being physically able to do her housework—situations that are difficult and likely to be chronic, our interviewees tended to believe that the older person belonged in an institution—if finances permitted. It appears, then, that living in a home for the aged is seen as a contingency arrangement when the finances can be handled and when independent living or family care is not possible.

The following areas of family relationships were also considered in the interview with Green Township and Pennsboro adults: the degree of autonomy that elderly parents should allow their grown children, the expectations of the degree to which grandmothers should interact with grandchildren, opinions about an older person's living frugally in order to leave money to his children, and the advisability of remarriage for older persons.

The idea that parents should allow grown children to lead their own lives had general support in the community. For example, nearly 60 percent of the respondents felt that grown children should not always be expected to come home on holidays, since they have plans of their own or their own children to consider. Lesser numbers felt that "It's nice for families to be together on holidays if everyone wants to come," but others said firmly, "Family gatherings are nice and everyone *should* come." In general, however, community members seemed to feel that family get-togethers are pleasant but that grown children should attend only if they wish or if it is convenient for them.

Concerning the desirability of older parents giving advice to their grown children, a quarter of the respondents said they thought such advice would help the children. However, 41 percent believed that parents should advise their grown children only when asked. Others felt that the question centered around the quality of the advice and the individuals involved. Apparently, the attitude is that grown children should not have to listen to their parents' advice, much less to accept it, and that they themselves should be able to decide when and on what topics advice might be sought. Thus the adult children would govern this intergenerational relationship.

When the study participants were asked whether grandmothers should enjoy being with their grandchildren, not quite half the group, begging the question, said that, indeed, most grandmothers do love their grandchildren. Twenty percent felt that grandmothers should enjoy their grandchildren but they shouldn't have the responsibility for them. Close to a third expressed the idea that if a grandmother does not want to be with her grandchildren, it's all right because "children sometimes get on an older person's nerves." In the grandmother-grandchildren relationship, then, autonomy is given to the grandmother to decide the extent to which she and the children are together.

Should an older person deprive himself in order to leave money to his children? The anecdote was as follows: "When Beth's husband died he left her fairly well off. But, rather than spend the money, she lives as cheaply as possible so she can pass it on to her children." Responding community members overwhelmingly said that an older person should spend his money to care for his own needs first. This was expressed in different ways: "Older parents need money more than their children do"; "They should take care of their own needs and the children can make their own way"; or "It's bad to live cheaply in order to save for the children." Some of the participants did comment, "A mother shouldn't deprive herself of the necessities, but it shows that she is thinking of the children's welfare," while others added a specific condition: "A mother shouldn't skimp unless the children are sick or disabled."

It would appear, then, that saving unnecessarily and depriving oneself in order to pass on money to children was generally not condoned in this community. It was felt that older persons should care for their own needs before those of their adult children, unless these children were handicapped in some way.

When an anecdote about remarriage for an older, widowed person was presented to the interviewees, over 80 percent replied that remarriage would be all right if this was what the older person wanted. Though considerations such as age, children, health, and finances were mentioned occasionally as matters to think about, less than 10 percent of the adults rejected the idea of remarriage for older persons. A few others expressed additional reservations. The norm seemed to be that the older person's judgment was generally respected and that his feelings mattered more than other considerations.

That various groups within our respondents differed in their views will be seen when we discuss what interviewee variables are associated with opinions expressed.

Participation in Community Life

The anecdotes used in assessing how Liberty County residents felt about older people participating in community affairs dealt with the need for older people to keep busy, their activities in helping others, organizations in the area that would accept older persons as members and officers, and the question of how much older and younger people should associate with each other.

The findings showed that over half of the respondents believed that older people should be active in community affairs, primarily because, as they said, "It's good for a person's state of mind to be in things," and, as another expressed it, "An older person should be active in the community because he needs to occupy his time." In contrast, less than 15 percent of the interviewees felt that older people should go into community activities for the reason that they could be of any help. This suggests that older people were seen generally as the beneficiaries of any good coming from their participation rather than because they held some special skills of value to the community.

This view can hardly be thought of as rejection of an older person's participation, however, since less than four percent of the respondents said they felt that "older people should stay out of things and let young people take over." In fact, sizable numbers suggested organizations that would welcome older persons as members and/or officers. Women tended to be favored somewhat over men for church work, while men were thought of in connection with lodges and the fire company; both men and women were suggested for service groups.

The participants supported the idea of association between the old and the young, but added such provisos as: "If the age groups can get along well together"; "If the younger people don't mind." In the replies of Liberty County adults there was a tendency to feel that much of the prerogative for interaction depends upon younger persons. Perhaps this is a bow to a democratic spirit in social organizations, but it may also be an additional expression that older persons have more to gain from such associations than do younger ones. As 25 percent said, "It does an older person good to be with younger people." Somewhat fewer, 19 percent, said, "It does younger people good to be with older people," but 6 percent rejected the idea of the two age groups being together, saying, "It's bad" or "It won't work out."

Solving Personal Problems

A fifth group of items pertained to the sources of help that members of the community felt older people should turn to if they had problems of loneliness, physical or mental illness, physical incapacity, or lack of money. The results show that respondents could name people and agencies within the community who they believed would help an older person with his problems, with the source of help depending largely upon the situation. Some suggestions were quite specific, and others were quite general. Answers to our anecdotal problem-solving questions were placed in these categories: the family, friends, the minister or religion, (other) professional persons, and an agency.

"An older person who is lonesome should find company in his friends and neighbors," said many; "The minister could help," said many others. "A couple almost out of money should get public assistance," said 68 percent of the interviewees. Physicians were the suggested sources of help for those with physical problems, but some said that imagination may be the problem.

Sources of help for those with problems of senility or mental illness were not so easily suggested by members of the community. To one anecdote, one-third replied that an older woman who acts "queer" should be taken to the doctor, 40 percent felt she should be sent to a home, and about a quarter believed that her family should assume responsibility for her care as best they can. Dependence of older people upon their families for help in case of financial need, and also in the case of physical inability to cope with housekeeping tasks, was thought appropriate by only small proportions of the respondents.

A number of statements indicate that there was a tendency for people in Pennsboro and Green Township to feel that a person with problems ought first to work out his own solution as best he can, using his own abilities and resources. Yes, family, friends, and professional persons could help, but only after one has tried to help himself. Self-sufficiency included, of course, the need to decide things oneself. For example, nearly 60 percent of the respondents felt that a woman who is physically unable to do her housework should hire some help. A lesser percentage believed that in such a case the woman should just let the jobs "go" or get a smaller place in which to live, but that she should still be responsible for herself.

How individuals solve their problems or how they help to solve those of others depends upon what resources are available—the kind of professional persons and organizations that can usefully serve them, directly or indirectly. It is said that services for older people in communities in the United States are much more scarce than elsewhere (see the report of the U.S. Senate Special Committee on Aging, 1961). To what extent were organizations and professional services actually oriented and used by older residents of Pennsboro and the rest of Green Township? During our 1955 field work, interviews were held with an officer of each of 28 community organizations (Appendix I), as well as with each of 21 professional or semiprofessional persons who conceivably could be assisting older individuals in the area (Appendix J). Of the 28 organizations contacted, five had over 20 members 65 years of age or older; for three groups this was over 25 percent of their membership. The representative of the local historical society said that 75 percent of its membership was in this age group. Only two informants mentioned programs planned especially for older persons, one (the University Extension Service) having held two meetings concerned with Social Security. Four said that their programs appealed to people of all ages.

The officers were asked to what extent older persons participated in the organization's affairs. One replied, "Just as much as anyone else"; another said, "About half of them are active." A representative of a political organization said, "The middle-aged group are the workers, but proper respect is given the older ones. They are asked to speak to the group at times." A Grange official said, "They hold offices. They are depended upon for counsel and guidance in making decisions."

The respondents were asked if there were any particular advantages that older persons bring to their organizations. All except three replied in the affirmative, and proceeded to mention positive attributes: "They have a rich historical knowledge." "They lend dignity and a certain maturity." "They lend a steadying influence." "They have experience." "They're always at home." "They bring in younger people, and if you win them they are the best advertisers." "They give us courage to live and work—inspiration!" One informant said, "When they're cooperative, they add maturity and experience."

Twenty of the 28 interviewees said that older persons presented no special problems to their organizations.

The special problems presented by older people were: "They are hard of hearing, unable to drive cars and to attend regularly." "There's the fear of falling," one said. Other problems were "their resistance to change," "their interests being different from younger members," and a "tendency to feel their contribution has already been made."

An inquiry was made of 21 professional persons' activities in relation to older people in Liberty County. This category included physicians, attorneys, insurance brokers, representatives of two social service agencies, the director of a nearby state mental hospital, the school superintendent, and ministers. Contacts with older adults varied, but usually they were under 10 percent of their clientele.

The findings indicate that for the most part organizational and professional services are not oriented particularly toward older adults. The attitude apparently was that older persons are free, along with everyone else, to enjoy whatever services are available. The services of professional persons were not in great demand by older persons; the one instance in which a social agency had been called upon by an older resident of our area was when a man sought help for his *grandchild*. At the time of this survey, social and psychiatric services were neither sought nor utilized by the old for themselves, and such help was more likely to be suggested by younger persons.

There were important variations in how subgroups within our study population viewed ways to solve problems, as well as how they viewed other areas of behavior for older persons. Let us turn to those analyses.

Opinions in Relation to Characteristics of Interviewees

While the opinions expressed above appear to reflect the attitudes of the adult respondents *generally*, it is important to note that groups within the community differed in the ideas they held concerning appropriate behavior for older persons. When 20 percent or more of the respondents expressed the same view concerning a question, the replies were cross-tabulated with characteristics of the respondents and analyzed for the statistical significance of differences. Use was made of such factors as age, sex, educational level, and occupational status of interviewees. These factors were interrelated, however. For example, as compared to older respondents, the younger respondents tended to be women, who also were often individuals belonging to families in which the wage earner held a higher status occupation.

The younger adults often tended significantly to feel that retirement should occur at a specific age; more than persons aged 60 or over, younger respondents felt a person should retire when he reached a certain age—usually between 60 and 70. Younger adults often tended significantly to approve remarriage for older persons, while the latter often saw problems connected with it. Younger interviewees also believed that older people should be active in the community, and they seemed to be better informed than their elders about possible groups that older people could join and participate in. Younger participants also offered more suggestions on ways in which an older person could solve his personal problems; they often favored seeking professional help for chronic difficulties rather than simply putting up with them or using family remedies.

Older adults, on the other hand, more frequently than younger ones, were likely to approve of a person working as long as he was physically able rather than specifying a definite age for retirement. The older interviewees seemed convinced that adult generations should live in separate quarters, but they also felt that it was a prerogative of parents to advise their grown children. Older participants were less likely than younger ones to believe that older persons should be active in the community, and they were also less aware of organizations that would welcome older people as members or officers.

Interviewees living in households where the wage earner was a professional, technical, or related worker were also the better-educated respondents. These participants tended to favor working as long as a person was physically able and, in general, they believed that activity on the older person's part was a good thing. They also condoned remarriage for widowed older people. Conversely, the respondents from lower occupational groups significantly often felt that retirement should occur at a specific age. The lower-status interviewees more than others also felt that it was all right for parents to advise their grown children. These persons were less certain of the value of activity for older people, offering more conditions for their participation than did better-educated and higher-status occupational groups.

THE REPUTATIONS OF
OLDER PERSONS IN THE COMMUNITY

Purpose

In addition to understanding some of the norms and expectations that the community held for its older people in general, we wished to learn how our older subjects were seen in the community—to learn about their *reputations*. We wanted to see how their reputations were or were not related to personal variables and to our measures of personality and adjustment. We defined *reputation* as the character commonly imputed to a person by others, as distinct from his "real" or nonpublic or more personal character. We hypothesized that older persons' reputations among other adults in Pennsboro and Green Township were related to their health, economic security, and leisure-time activities as well as to our measures of their personality and adjustment.

Procedure

As previously described, in the house-to-house survey in 1955, an adult in each household was interviewed concerning behavioral norms and expectations for older people. He was asked to suggest appropriate solutions to problems of older persons, and then asked, "Do you know some older person around here who is getting along well in his retirement? Anyone else?" Also: "Do you know some older person around here with good living arrangements, who is getting along well with his family?" The respondent was also asked to name older individuals he knew were *not* getting along so well in these areas. Thus, each respondent could make free choices of persons 65 years of age or over living in the community who were "getting along well" and "not getting along so well." The procedure was similar to that used in the "guess who" technique of sociometric studies (Lindzey and Byrne, 1968).

Each of the 487 respondents, therefore, had an opportunity to name, either positively or negatively, older persons in the community with reference to each area of social norms. Seventy-five percent of the respondents mentioned some older person in the study community. In absolute numbers, there were more women in the community 65 years of age and older to be nominated, so it is not surprising that more women than men were so named.

Reputation Ratings

Our attention at this moment is to those subjects who were willing and able to be interviewed in 1956—59 men and 87 women (Table 20). (Later we shall concern ourselves with the longitudinal subjects, those interviewed in 1956, 1962, and 1965, whose Reputation Ratings were shown in Table 12.) Of these 146 persons, 101, or 70 percent were mentioned in reply to our request for names of older persons getting along well or not so well. As shown in Table 29, men and women were mentioned about equally often—73 and 67 percent, respectively. Sixteen of our older men and 28 of the older women subjects were not mentioned at all by other adults in the community.

The ways in which each older person was mentioned were tabulated, and judges evaluated the positive or negative character of the ways in which people were mentioned. The correlations between two judges' ratings was .95, indicating almost complete agreement. Forty-seven percent of both men and women were mentioned positively, 19 percent were mentioned negatively, and the remaining one-third were mentioned in a neutral way.

TABLE 29

Frequency of Older Persons Being Mentioned and Their
Reputation Ratings, 1956 Interviewees, by Percent

	Men		Women	
Item	N	%	N	%
Older persons				
Mentioned	43	73	58	67
Not mentioned	16	27	29	33
Total	59	100	87	100
Reputation ratings				
Positive (5-7)	20	47	27	47
Neutral (4)	16	37	19	33
Negative (1-3)	7	16	12	20
Total	43	100	58	100

Relation of Reputations to Other Variables

To learn whether reputations of older adults were related to such variables as age, education, health, and marital happiness, correlations were obtained between the Reputation Ratings and other variables. These correlations are shown in Table 30. These

TABLE 30

Correlations[a] of Reputation Ratings with Selected
Variables, for 1956 Interviewees

Variable	Men (N = 43)[a]	Women (N = 58)[a]
Age	25	07
Education	14	15
Occupational status	10	12
Employment status	−03	16
Self-rating on health	39	43
Happiness of (last) marriage	11	11
Number of leisure activities	36	21
Self-rating of economic position	32	28
Frequency of church attendance	39	11

[a]Pearson product-moment correlations, decimals omitted; N's vary according to data available.

findings indicated that, although the relationships between reputations and other variables were not great, some associations were
moderate. The highest correlations for both men and women
concerned self-ratings on health and economic position. Some sex
differences were evident, as in the case of older men, where
modest relationships were found between reputation and the
number of leisure activities and frequency of church attendance.

Relation of Reputation Ratings to Other Measures

Table 31 presents correlations between measures of personality and adjustment of older subjects and the Reputation Ratings.
Again, although correlations were low, there appears to be some
positive association between older persons' reputations (and how
active they were) and how they felt about themselves, as well as
how community members had evaluated them. Judges who rated
interview material tended to agree with the reputations of older
adults, as shown by correlations of .49 for men and .41 for
women. A correlation of .47 between the Reputation Rating and
the Community Rating showed a moderate relationship between

TABLE 31

Correlations[a] of Reputation Ratings with Measures
of Personality and Adjustment
for 1956 Interviewees

Measure	Men (N = 43)[a]	Women (N = 58)[a]
Activity Inventory	38	29
Attitude Inventory	32	28
Judge's Rating	49	41
Personal Relations and Sociability Scale	32	20
Thematic Apperception Test	23	16
Opinion Conformity Scale	14	04
Interviewer's Rating	28	−09
Community Rating (Q)	− 47	−

[a]Pearson product-moment correlations, decimals omitted; N's
vary according to data available.

two evaluations external to the individual—one by adults who had a free choice and the other by selected panelists who followed the special forced-choice, Q-sort procedure (to be described in detail in the next section). Interviewer's ratings did not agree very well with the reputations. The element of free choice in the reputation measure is pertinent, for adult interviewees undoubtedly responded to our request only by naming individuals whose identity they could, without much guilt, reveal. Though 75 percent of the adult interviewees did in fact make nominations, they often expressed reluctance to name names, thinking it unnecessary and even undesirable to do so. In addition, the fact that older persons in Pennsboro and Green Township were simply not known to other adults in the community is also relevant. The geographical area is fairly large (approximately 30 square miles), and individuals can apparently remain quite anonymous within it. Some indirect evidence bearing on this question is to be derived from our use of the Community Rating technique.

All correlations that concerned background variables and measures of personality and adjustment and reputation ratings of older persons were relatively low and accounted for rather little of the variance. Though personality, adjustment, and reputation were related, no one variable was highly correlated with the Reputation Rating. This may mean that, for older adults, reputations may be highly specific to them as individuals, and that community members consider a number of variables when they think of who is or is not managing well in old age. They did tend to view people getting along well in one area—say, family relations or living arrangements—as doing well in others, thus showing a "halo effect" in the nominations. It was apparent, as we indicated earlier, that different groups of adult respondents held different expectations for older persons, so it would be reasonable to expect that different segments of respondents nominated persons who differed in social and personality and adjustment variables.

Continuity and Change in Relation to Reputations

Here the question is: How is reputation in the community related to change or consistency over time? To find the answer we used our longitudinal subjects only—the 17 men and 29 women who were interviewed and tested in 1956, 1962, and 1965. Their

Reputation Ratings, also derived from the survey of 1955, were presented in Table 12, where we describe these subjects in detail. That table showed that 59 percent of the men and 71 percent of the women were mentioned in terms of reputation. The men had a higher mean Reputation Rating than women, 5.10 compared to 3.76; women varied somewhat more than the men. The numbers, of course, are small: 10 men and 21 women.

Change was shown primarily in terms of Longitudinal Trend Scores. When we compared subjects whose average LTS's indicated some improvement over the years with those whose scores showed decline, in relation to their reputation ratings we found the following: four of the six "improvers" (those with positive LTS's) had ratings of 5 or higher, while two had ratings of 4 or lower; of the 22 "decliners" (those with negative LTS's), 11 were in the higher reputation category and 11 were in the lower category. Thus, our Reputation Rating is not a good predictor of change in personality and adjustment.

Survival in Relation to Reputations

How good a predictor of survival is reputation? Does knowledge of the positive or negative character of an older person's reputation have any value in predicting his or her death or survival? These data, presented in Table 26, indicate that knowledge of reputation, at least as we measured it, did not assist in predicting death or survival.

In our study of the place of older persons in a small rural community we selected a special group to study more intensively. We shall now describe our procedure and discuss these findings.

COMMUNITY RATINGS—PEER-GROUP EVALUATIONS

Purpose

From the beginning of our research on personality and adjustment of older adults, we pondered the question of how the types of measures commonly used by psychologists would correspond to some real-life criteria that a person's peers might use in evaluating him. The Reputation Rating provided something of an answer, but we wanted a better one. We began to ask ourselves: How closely would results from methods we had selected, and were devising for use in an interviewing situation with the older adults, agree with findings from a procedure involving people who saw them function in the daily life of a community? This is essentially a problem of determining validity, of learning how "truthfully" a procedure assesses an attribute, as compared to another procedure.

Procedure

The techniques we worked out to obtain peer-group evaluations took advantage of the small community in which individuals had a reasonably good chance of being rather widely known. They were based upon the assumption that members of the community could appraise other persons they knew according to ability to function appropriately and effectively in the life of their community. We necessarily had to find "peers" who could and would make useful appraisals, and we had to identify which of our older subjects could be appraised. And, of course, we had to have a means to obtain the judgments. We shall describe our methods in that order.

Selection of Community Raters

The selection of judges followed several criteria. To qualify as a judge of persons aged 65 and over, we arbitrarily said that a person could not himself be 65 or over and thereby also be eligible as a subject. Further, a judge had to be someone with whom the investigators could communicate the rationale of seeking such information and how we intended to obtain it. It was necessary for us to determine in advance whether or not the individual would cooperate with us (over the years) and, equally important, whether or not he could and would do the task effectively. This meant that we expected reasonably objective judgments from persons who were relatively noncontroversial figures in the community.

In the process of selecting potential judges, we explained this phase of our work to several community consultants. They were generally the same individuals who had helped us in liaison and in the launching of the project (Chapter 2). They readily provided us with the names of persons they thought were equal to the task and whose evaluations would be useful. Our 1955 community survey data provided us with other candidates for community raters. In all, 31 persons were so nominated—nine men and 22 women (Table 32).

TABLE 32

Information Concerning Selection of "Q-Subjects"
and Community Raters, by Number

Item	Men	Women	Total
Community Raters			
Nominated as raters	9	22	31
Knew maximum number of subjects	6	11	17
Completed the ratings	5	11	16
Ratings agreed with others	3	9	12
"Q-Subjects"			
Living and in area in 1956	68	108	176
Interviewed in 1956	59	87	146
Attitude Inventory completed	56	85	141
Known well by maximum number of raters ("Eligible Q's")	11	30	41
Stratified, random sample (Q Ss)	5	20	25

We had already identified our potential subjects—in fact, this part of the study followed closely the initial interviewing of our older subjects in 1956. We needed to determine how well qualified the judge nominees were in terms of how many of the subjects they knew. The names and addresses of all 176 residents aged 65 and over—68 men and 108 women—were put on cards, and each nominated judge was asked to sort them into three categories: those he knew well, those he knew casually, and those he knew not at all. These responses for the 31 nominees were tabulated, and then the nominees were eliminated one by one according to how many older people they knew. Some who had been nominated simply did not know enough people to qualify; for example, one young minister who had recently moved to the community knew his own older parishioners casually but most others not at all. The process of elimination involved arriving at a balance of "knowers" with the "known," at maximum numbers for each. Seventeen (six men and 11 women) of the 31 men and women qualified by knowing a maximum number of subjects. In a second interview these persons were asked to evaluate the sample of 25 subjects, and 16 of the 17 completed the task. One man tried and tried to do what we asked, but finally gave up in exasperation, saying in all sincerity, "The good Lord says, 'Thou shalt not judge,' and I just can't do it. I can't do it!"

To learn how well the 16 judges agreed with each other on their appraisals, we correlated the scores derived from their evaluations of the 25 subjects in each of the five areas with the 16-judge total for the respective area. Mean correlations of each judge with the total were obtained, which we viewed as "consistency coefficients." Of the 16 consistency coefficients, 12 were above .60, a criterion we set arbitrarily. The evaluations of these 12 were used for the Community Rating of 1956, and the appraisals of the remaining four judges were dropped from the analysis. The 1956 ratings, then, were made by 12 judges: three men and nine women. For the subsequent years of evaluation, including those of the longitudinal subjects, the same judges were used, when available, and only those from whom ratings had been secured at all three points in the data collection were finally used. The Community Ratings used for the longitudinal subjects were made each year by 6 judges: two men and four women.

In 1956 the 12 judges providing the Community Rating had a mean age of 45.5 years. All had lived in the Pennsboro area for ten years or more. One-half were employed, and these were in professional or managerial positions. Except for one, all had completed high school and five had completed college.

Selection of Q-Subjects

To qualify as a *subject* for this community panel analysis, our older subjects must have been able and willing to be interviewed in our 1956 wave. These persons numbered 146—83 percent of those eligible (Table 20). Of the 146, nearly all (141) completed the Attitude Inventory in the course of our interview, as shown in Table 32. The criterion of having the Attitude Inventory score on each subject followed our desire to have at least minimal data available as a corollary measure.

Of course, it was necessary also that the subjects of our panel analysis be known well by the raters. Just as we eliminated some nominated judges for not knowing potential subjects, we eliminated potential subjects who were not known by enough judges. Eventually we arrived at a maximum number of subjects known by a maximum number of raters. Thus, 11 men and 30 women, a total of 41, were selected as eligible subjects—about 20 percent of the men and 35 percent of the women who were otherwise qualified. Having more women than men suggested as judges in the first place, and more women who knew the maximum number of subjects, undoubtedly influenced the sex differential in those who became eligible for the Community Rating.

The final step in selecting subjects for the panel analysis was based upon our desire to have as heterogenous a group of subjects as we could on the measures of personality and adjustment that we obtained directly from the subjects. Since the Attitude Inventory scores were available, we made a frequency distribution of them for the 41 eligible subjects. We had arbitrarily decided that 25 was the maximum number of subjects the panelists could evaluate by means of our method. We therefore divided the distribution into fifths and then randomly selected five subjects from each fifth. They numbered five men and 20 women, whom we referred to as the Q-subjects, since the procedure we followed involved a Q-sort.

With one or two exceptions, these 25 subjects are quite like the 146 subjects from whom they were selected. In terms of age, occupational status, and self-rating on health, the distributions are quite similar. One important difference, already mentioned, is the sex distribution. Since the Q-subjects included proportionally more women, there were proportionally more widows and, as it happened, more who had never married; hence, corresponding differences appeared in terms of living arrangements. The Q-group also included somewhat larger proportions of older persons who were better educated and in better economic circumstances than the original group of 146.

Thus, this special sample of subjects constituted a select group, select because they were well-known older adults, visible ones generally, but not necessarily well liked or popular. Our procedure had brought this selection about.[2]

Rating Procedure

In a personal interview each judge was asked to evaluate the Q-subjects on five dimensions relevant to their actual functioning in the life of the community: the respect others had for them, the value of their opinion, the extent to which they did what they were supposed to do, how considerate or helpful they were of others, and the number of friends they had (Appendix K). The names and addresses of subjects had been placed on cards, and the judge was to divide the cards into scale categories. In front of him we placed a long card in the form of a five-point rating scale, which included the number of cards to be placed in each category. For example, this scale was used:

A. He is unusually considerate of others.
B. He is helpful to others most of the time.
C. He will help when asked.
D. He helps others only when it's to his advantage.
E. He hardly ever helps anyone.

In 1956 the judge placed three, five, nine, five, and three in each such category, respectively; in 1962, three, four, seven, four, and three; in 1965, two, four, six, four, and two. The total was determined by the number still living and in the area. After he had done this for one dimension, the interviewer recorded the file numbers of subjects so arranged and then shuffled the subject cards for evaluation on the next dimension (see Appendix L).

Thus the judge was forced to distribute the subjects along five continua according to a "normal" distribution with five categories. Development of this forced-distribution procedure, based upon the Q-sort methods of Stevenson (1953), followed pilot work that indicated the lay judges' reluctance to distribute their choices

---

[2] In retrospect we believe that our selection procedures were quite adequate, given the task and setting, except with regard to sex. Future attempts should consider controlling this variable for selecting judges and subjects, but doing this should not preclude the possibility of cross-sex judgments.

adequately enough to enable discrimination. Once the Q-sort task was presented, our judges proceeded quite easily to complete it. We did not ask them to explain reasons for their placements, and reasons were seldom volunteered. Occasional questions arose, such as what standard should be employed—what the subject was like some years ago or what he was like now. To this question we replied that we were interested in how the judge saw him now. Our raters generally found the sorting task interesting but taxing, probably stemming from feelings of guilt at having to judge negatively, but they generally expressed the idea that they were glad to help us. Such interviews usually lasted less than an hour, except for the initial one, when we gathered other information from and about the rater himself.

The items were scored from five to one, A through E respectively. An individual's score was the sum of five ratings given by all six judges; the total possible score, then, was five scales $\times$ five points = 25 $\times$ six judges = 150. The distributions of the Community Rating scores for the longitudinal Q-subjects were presented in Table 14.

Intercorrelations among the five subscores for the 1956 Community Rating for the 25 subjects and 12 raters ranged from .49 to .85, all positive and statistically significant. Correlations of subscores with the total (part-whole correlations) averaged .89. The total score for the total number of raters was used for this measure.

Findings and Discussion

Our objective was to learn how peer-group evaluations of personality and adjustment correspond to evaluations made by other techniques. The analysis, using correlations with our 1956 subjects, is presented in Table 33. The correlations account for relatively little of the variance, in any case. Community Ratings correlated similarly with ratings made by judges (who assessed them through their interview material) and with their reputations in the wider community. Interviewers and community raters tended not to agree. The correlation with the Opinion Conformity Scale was negative, indicating that the more conforming the individual was to Liberty County norms the lower the community raters appraised him. Apparently the evaluators valued "deviating" thinkers to some extent.

TABLE 33

Correlations[a] of Community Rating with Other Measures
of Personality and Adjustment, 1956 Q-Subjects

Measure	Correlation
Activity Inventory	27
Attitude Inventory	25
Judge's Rating	50
Personal Relations and Sociability Scale	25
Thematic Apperception Test	80
Opinion Conformity Scale	−48
Interviewer's Rating	14
Reputation Rating (1955)	47

[a]Pearson product-moment correlations, decimals omitted;
N = 22, except for Reputation Rating, when N = 21.

The highest correlation was between the Community Rating and the TAT. As we explained in Chapter 3, the TAT's were assessed according to how the subject perceived the adequacy of the older person in the stories. This correlation of .80 indicated that persons who were seen favorably by their peers tended to see older adults as dynamic, effective, well regarded and capable. We repeat that we have viewed our TAT data quite skeptically, but this finding underscores the need for further exploration of the relationships between such outer manifestations of behavior as those inherent in the appraisals by other adults in the community and such inner manifestations as those assessed by projective instruments.

Except for this last finding, our data seem to show that, for the most part, objective-type tests, as exemplified by the Activity Inventory, the Attitude Inventory, and the P + S Scales, measure behavior that is not usually displayed publicly—in interview situations or in the daily life of the community. It would be useful to learn how true this would be if those judging an individual's functional behavior were explicitly seen by that individual as significant and important in his life, as individuals whose opinions and respect mattered deeply to him. Such a study of the "reference groups" of individuals should account for the changes that occur with time in the groups that he could potentially belong to, as well as changes that take place over a period of time in the individual himself. There is a dearth of such social-psycho-logical-developmental knowledge concerning all age periods, but especially concerning those throughout adult life.

In Chapter 3 we presented the Community Ratings for the 14 Q-subjects who were also subjects for our change-over-time analysis (Table 14). For this group there was some slight decline in the mean ratings over the nine-year period, but great consistency in how individuals were ranked within the group by the panelists (inter-year correlations, Table 15). Our analyses of Longitudinal Trend Scores for the Community Ratings, showing *individual* change in this measure, indicated that three subjects improved over the years in their Community Ratings, two remained about the same, and nine declined (Table 18, combined distribution). Decline was especially common among the women.

In regard to the standing of subjects on the Community Rating in relation to *survival*, over the years of the study we obtained data, comparable to the data shown in Tables 21, 22, and 23, on each of the Q-group subjects. Comparing (cumulatively) Q-subjects with non-Q-subjects, we note the following: in 1962, three of the 25 Q-subjects (12 percent) had died, in contrast to 87 of the 180 non-Q-subjects (48 percent); in 1965, seven of the Q's (28 percent) had died, compared to 109 of the non-Q's (61 percent); in 1967, eight of the Q's (32 percent) had died, in contrast to 120 of the non-Q-subjects (67 percent); by 1969, eight of the Q's (32 percent) had died, compared with 130 of the non-Q-subjects (72 percent); and after two more years, by July 1, 1971, 12 of the 25 Q-subjects (48 percent) had died, in contrast to 148 of the non-Q-subjects (82 percent). Thus, the subjects for the Community Rating appear to be a special group in several ways, including survival.

When the surviving Q-subjects were compared statistically (using the Fisher Exact Probability Test; Siegel, 1956) with those who had died, no significant differences in the Community Ratings were evident in any of the comparative years. While the subjects selected and evaluated by our community panelists did seem to be an especially hardy group, the surviving ones did not differ from nonsurviving ones on the original 1956 Community Rating.

Is *change* in Community Rating predictive of survival or nonsurvival? To provide clues to an answer on this question, we compared surviving and nonsurviving longitudinal subjects on whom we had Longitudinal Trend Scores for the Community Rating. Consistently the surviving subjects received higher ratings by community panelists, but the numbers of subjects so compared were so small that this finding must be viewed with caution.

THE SMALL RURAL COMMUNITY AS A PLACE TO LIVE AND AGE

The Idealized Small Community

In spite of growing urbanization and the decline of strictly "rural" cultural values, substantial proportions of American elderly still live in communities classified as rural, farm, or nonfarm. Moreover, the small town, often predominantly rural in its value system, had been idealized as a place for the elderly to live out their post-retirement years. It seems appropriate that we should put together our impressions of "our" rural community as a place in which to live and grow old. We do this now, basing some of our thoughts on data we have gathered and basing others on what we and our field workers experienced as we went about the community and talked with people. We believe that in spite of our sincere respect—even affection—for the Pennsboro and Green Township area and their residents, we could see both the unpleasant and pleasant features clearly and objectively! We add, too, that we are frankly skeptical about the rural-urban dimension as a variable that is very important in differentiating individual behavior, a point we have raised elsewhere (Britton and Britton, 1967).

The Community as a Primary Group

During the period of our study, the community of Pennsboro and Green Township was basically one with a primary group orientation, with families intermarrying and linked together by familial ties and experiences over long periods of time. Although some younger adults in the community moved away, the community was stable, with many long-time residents. Relationships seemed to be characterized by fairly frequent and easy contact among residents, especially within their respective groups and associations; there was friendliness among acquaintances and reserved, sometimes even suspicious, attitudes toward strangers.

These characteristics appeared to offer a measure of safety, especially for the elderly. People were known and observed, and they seemed to be concerned for others. Often, in attempting to locate older subjects, interviewers would inquire of neighbors, merchants, or officials as to their whereabouts. It was not unusual to learn, "Oh, sure, I saw her this morning"; "Yes, he came in to shop. His sister's sick"; "No, you won't find him at home today. His daughter took him with her in the car." A store clerk volunteered to an interviewer, "I wouldn't bother Mrs. X right now. She always takes a nap right after lunch."

Habits and routines of many residents seemed to be well known, and it was noticed when usual patterns were broken. One woman expressed her own feeling of security after her daughter, who lives down the street, called her one morning and asked if she was all right. Assured that she was, the daughter replied, "I saw that the shade in your bedroom window wasn't raised this morning and I was worried."

While some observers might abhor this lack of privacy, many old people expressed a feeling of comfort, knowing they were "checked upon" and their comings and goings noted. Likewise they themselves felt that knowing what others were doing added interest to their lives.

This kind of neighborliness was undoubtedly characteristic of some people far more than of others, and certainly does not imply that nearly all contact was intimate or congenial. In fact, some behavior of the sort we have described appeared quite superficial. Some of it could have been motivated by hostile or envious curiosity or by "nosiness."

We do not feel that neighborliness is restricted to the small rural community. Within large urban areas we have observed that residents often know other dwellers' routines and assist them in friendly and helpful ways. The complicating factor in the urban setting would appear to be the apparent impersonality imposed on the system by the many other persons who enter and leave the vicinity without regular or apparent contact with others in it.

Social Norms

In Pennsboro and Green Township a variety of behavior was condoned, as evidenced from our study of social norms. This fact may have made it a more comfortable place to live than one which was more rigid and restricting. In the area of family relationships, for example, older family members appeared to be valued for their wisdom and experience; their help and companionship were appreciated, at least to some degree. The older adult was seen as being able to look after himself and he was usually expected to do so. Still, there was a willingness, particularly within the family, for the people to help each other, old or young, in case of need. Unless they needed help, however, adult generations in a family were expected to be quite autonomous.

On the other hand, our normative data showed that community members encouraged older people to seek governmental or institutionalized help such as public assistance rather than to assure them that family or friends would take care of their problem. This suggests that residents felt that other agencies function better than primary groups in certain arenas, especially in matters involving money. Thus, one could sense what seemed sometimes to be an indifferent "I don't care what they do" attitude that was contradicted, perhaps, by the feeling that one's taxes, after all, took care of this kind of help and hence it was one's *right* to expect it. It appeared to us that adults felt their prime obligation was to their progeny rather than to the generation that preceded them, and that the old recognized this priority almost as often as did the young.

Throughout our study of the expectations that community adults had for the behavior of older people, the themes of autonomy, independence, and self-sufficiency appeared to be strong. While both younger and older adults stressed this, the meaning of self-sufficiency might be seen quite differently by the two groups. This was poignantly apparent in the data concerning the solving of personal problems. To younger adults, self-sufficiency seemed to mean "Take care of yourself as long as possible and then turn to a professional person for advice or an institution for care"; to the older person, however, self-sufficiency often signified "Take care of yourself as long as you can and then your family should help." Both generations agreed in part, but were potentially in conflict if and when the ideal failed. If older persons are unaware (as we believe they often are) of nonfamily sources of help in times of need, such views of others, especially by the members of one's family, may produce anxiety, frustration, and conflict.

Other findings give further indications of the quality of Liberty County as a place in which to grow old. Generally, participation in community affairs was favored for all citizens, with the elderly free to participate for the good it would do them and for the help they can give to their organizations. Organizational leaders seemed to welcome older members, along with all the rest, although few, if any, special provisions were made for the elderly. We think this is indicative of an absence of "age-grading" among adults in most community affairs, and in this respect our community may be similar to the small town Barker and Wright called "Midwest." Their findings concerning social participation indicated that

> . . . the need for participants was so great in relation to the number of inhabitants that selection on the basis of sex, age, social group, intelligence, personality, political beliefs, or wealth was virtually impossible. . . . [This] lack of segregation . . . was a factor adding to the richness of life for Midwest [residents]. . . . The old and the young, the rich and the poor, the bright and the dull rubbed shoulders in most settings" (Barker and Wright, 1954, p. 460).

Barker and Gump (1964) and their associates drew similar conclusions in *Big School, Small School*: "A school should be sufficiently small that all its students are needed for its enterprises . . . [so] that students are not redundant" (p. 202).

It is quite possible that the lack of provision for the special needs of elderly persons indicates a real indifference toward their being actively involved in the community. However, because such needs—be they due to inability to walk or to climb stairs, or to see or to hear, or whatever—are idiosyncratic, and because in any one setting they pertain to so few persons, this may preclude the kind of organized efforts of accommodation that association officers could refer to in our survey. We believe this indicates less sheer indifference than the feeling that in old age one expects these things to occur and that individuals and organizations and even whole communities have to put up with them as best they can. And besides, many (but not all) organizational leaders seemed to feel that participation by the elderly was mostly for their own benefit rather than for that of others.

Social Change

Although Pennsboro is a rather self-contained community, it cannot be said to be isolated from the social changes that affect most communities. Technological changes are creating new expectations of what constitutes the desirable. New definitions of personal comfort and new standards of living involving expectations of both material and nonmaterial comfort are emerging. The value placed on efficiency coupled with the increasing belief in specialized knowledge, and faith in the technical expert's ability to provide solutions to problems, be they nonhuman or human, have an impact upon the attitudes and values of the people of Liberty County.

We believe these changes are affecting the lives of all residents, including the old. For example, while kinship patterns are still strong among the residents of Pennsboro and Green Township, privacy and the freedom to pursue individual activities are becoming important values in family life. The idea of a three-generation household is less accepted now by both adult generations because of the belief that privacy contributes to comfort and well-being and even to individual development within the family. This seems to occur in spite of higher standards of living that provide more equipment and more space for specialized activities in the home. There is also less obligation for family members to spend holidays together. Thus, there seems to be an increasing belief in the right to independence and in individuals' judging for themselves what is best for them.

Our impressions include another indicator of such secularism: the tendency to feel that it is no more efficient for each family to care for its older members than for each family to provide for the education of its young. This is obviously related to the fact that it seems increasingly possible economically for families to provide such care; due to current inflationary trends in the economy, however, this tendency may not be extended. With the advent of more adequate, nationally funded, and universally applicable forms of economic support and health care for the elderly, new attitudes about the economic security and independence of older people may well arise. Associated with these changes, we predict, will be further shifts in views about responsibility and its division between and among the individual, his family, a corporation (such as the company for which he worked), and a governmental body. Thus the norms for independence and self-sufficiency will become increasingly complex and deal with more dimensions than is true now.

The influence of social change may be expressed in other attitudes about interdependence along kinship lines. Perhaps ideally a person should no longer have to depend upon kinsmen or neighbors for assistance, nor ideally be obligated to extend assistance to them. With the availability of more technical equipment, the sharing of work and the borrowing of equipment among families and neighbors are becoming less frequent. People are more often expected to provide their own materials and tools and to rely upon themselves rather than "impose" upon family members or friends for either material equipment or help. For many older people this new attitude is foreign to the basic notion of kinship—the mutuality of helpfulness. This is confounded somewhat by the tendency of younger people to value work and aid in economic terms rather than as the performance of kinship or friendship obligations. Thus the attitude was expressed to us by some Libery County adults that if an older woman became unable physically to do her housework, the *ideal* solution would be to hire someone to help rather than to depend upon family or neighbors. In that way, it was implied, there would be no need to add up the count to make sure that each family member did his share of helping or that each neighbor contributed equally.

As we have mentioned, another tendency among younger, better educated, higher-status members of the community was to depend upon outside agencies and professional services and advice by experts rather than upon the family in the solution of problems. Older people appeared to be less willing to accept this view, and they seemed to express some bewilderment at the notion that families should have less to offer people in their problems than an outside agent. Thus there is a disparity between the old idea that an older person who is becoming senile needs the comfort and assistance of his family and the new faith that what he needs is a psychiatrist or a bed in a convalescent home.

There are other ways in which social change in Liberty County affects the lives of its older people. Our impression is that a shift in the assignment of status is occurring: from ascription on the basis of age, sex, or social class to that based on achievement. Though allowances are made for age, evaluations and assignment of status are more often made in terms of *present* rather than past achievements and contributions. Thus, when asked about how much weight an older officer's opinion would carry in an organization, some adults expressed the idea that these would have to be evaluated along with those of others. With an increase in reliance upon the expert with technical knowledge, the experience of the elders does not automatically apply and their status position is in jeopardy. Thus, for the Liberty County elderly, status is not assured unless they continue to achieve well and unless their talents continue to be needed. We suspect that this potential loss of status will be tempered by other factors—financial power, for example, or attractive personal characteristics. We also believe that there will continue to be positions in organizations that middle-aged or younger adults will not compete for, and that in some organizations, such as historical societies, age may even be an advantage.

SUMMARY

This chapter offers no clear-cut assessment of the small rural community as an ideal place in which to age. Our impression that there is a growth in the community of such potentially negative tendencies as attitudes of impersonality, a reduction of kinship ties, obligations, and privileges, an overvaluation of efficiency, specialization, and self-sufficiency, as well as of a high degree of individual autonomy for adults, should be regarded tentatively. Whether these values will become dominant ones in Liberty County, or become sufficiently strong to affect all or almost all residents, remains to be seen. Furthermore, increased affluence and increased dependence on institutionalized solutions to personal problems will undoubtedly lead to more technical services for the aged and to more concern for their material comfort. If these advances can be linked with a growing appreciation of older people as persons, who enjoy, along with all others, real places in the social scheme of the community, we would view Pennsboro and Green Township as a more optimal community in which to grow old.

Chapter 6

Summary and Interpretation

OBJECTIVES OF THE RESEARCH

The purpose of this research was to study some of the behavioral processes of aging by observing them developmentally, as change over time, among persons living in their own homes in a community where most had lived all their lives. In this research, personality and adjustment were defined as both personal (or "inner") and social (or "outer") in their dimensions. More specifically, we attempted to study the following:

1. Changes in the personalities of older adults over a period of time, the adjustment to aging they were able to make, and the factors related to change or consistency.

2. Problems of survivorship among older adults, with social-psychological correlates of survival being obtained by analyzing the differences between survivors and nonsurvivors.

3. Social norms and expectations for the behavior of older persons by other members of the community.

THE SETTING AND THE SUBJECTS

The setting for the study was a Pennsylvania village and the surrounding township: "Pennsboro" and "Green Township" in "Liberty County" (Chapter 2). This community is the center of an agricultural area and is more or less typical of rural and rural nonfarm areas in Pennsylvania. Approximately 10 percent of the population of 2,000 was aged 65 and over, and all men and women in the area in this age group were listed as potential subjects for the study.

The first phase of the investigation consisted of a house-to-house survey in order to locate all persons aged 64 years of age and older. At this time information was also collected from an adult in each household (N = 487) concerning the social norms and community expectations for older persons.

By means of the house-to-house census, 205 persons aged 64 or over were located in 1955. A year later, in 1956, 176 persons aged 65 and over were still living and residing in the community, of whom 146 were willing and able to be interviewed in 1956; they are subjects for portions of the analyses—for example, some of those dealing with survivorship. Of these 146 individuals, 46—17 men and 29 women—survived the nine-year period of the study of continuity and change and were interviewed and tested on all three occasions: 1956, 1962, and 1965. These persons have been referred to as the "longitudinal subjects." At the first assessment, about half of them were between the ages of 65 and 69; at the third assessment, nearly three-fourths were between 75 and 84 years of age. All were native-born white, generally Anglo-Saxon and Protestant in background. While about one-third of the men and nearly half of the women had not attended high school, as a group our subjects were somewhat better educated than older persons generally in the United States. In addition, nearly all the longitudinal subjects might be characterized as being middle class and native to the Liberty County area. Many of the men had been owners and operators of small or medium-sized farms or of businesses. A sample of subjects was evaluated by selected community residents in order to learn how commonly used psychological assessment procedures compared with community members' assessments. These panelists used a Q-sort procedure, and we called this sample the "Q-subjects."

THE PROCEDURE

Interviewers making the house-to-house census of Pennsboro and Liberty County in 1955 used a schedule that included open-ended and anecdotal questions (Appendix C). In 1956 each older adult was interviewed and tested individually in his own home. Follow-up sessions were held with all those surviving and still able and willing to be interviewed again in 1962 and in 1965. Statistical comparisons of successive "waves" of survivors and nonsurvivors have been made of these subjects, using baseline data from the 1955 survey and from the 1956 interviews, including background data and measures of personality and adjustment.

A variety of measures was used to assess personality and adjustment. Some were used directly with the individual himself; some sought information from others about him. Personality and adjustment involved older persons' activities, their attitudes toward themselves and their activities, their attitudes toward other persons, and the attitudes of others toward them. The measures were the following:

1. The *Chicago Activity Inventory* (devised by Burgess, Cavan, and Havighurst) uses objective questions concerning actual participation in various personal and social activities and concerning health problems.

2. The *Chicago Attitude Inventory*, constructed by Burgess, Cavan, and Havighurst, has been used widely in studies of the aged; it measures satisfaction with the ordinary activities of life and general feelings of happiness and usefulness.

3. The *Judge's Rating*, devised by Cavan, obtains judgments of an individual's behavior as revealed in interview material, in terms of his satisfaction with social relationships and his attitudes toward self.

4. The *Personal Relations (P) and Sociability (S) Scale* from the Guilford-Zimmerman Temperament Survey measures attitudes toward relations with older persons and general interest in and enjoyment of other persons. Some of the P and S items were adapted for our use.

5. Three cards (6BM, 7BM, and 10) from the *Thematic Apperception Test* were used to measure older adults' attitudes toward themselves. Each of the pictures included an older person; in the analysis of the stories, the main older person in the story was evaluated—for example, in terms of his adequacy in initiating action, his self-confidence, intellectual functioning, and interpersonal acceptance.

6. The *Opinion Conformity Scale* was based on the 1955 information on the community's expectations *for* older adults. It measured older persons' agreement with the predominant opinions of the community.

7. A *Reputation Rating* was obtained in connection with our 1955 survey, when we asked adults to identify older persons who were managing well or not so well in their everyday affairs.

8. The *Community Rating* provides an evaluation by selected residents of a sample of the subjects. The panelists used a Q-sort procedure to rate subjects on five aspects of their functioning in the community: respect, value of opinion, conformity, consideration for others, and friendships.

9. The *Interviewer's Rating* was based on his direct observa-

tion of the subject's ability to interact, see, hear, and cooperate in the interview situation.

SUMMARY OF THE FINDINGS

Continuity and Change

The mean age of both men and women subjects was about 71 at the first assessment and 80 at the last. The men rated their health less favorably than did the women; however, the group as a whole maintained a rather stable state of health. Likewise, marital status and living arrangements changed little for the subjects, except that they reduced their contact with family members over the years. As a group, the men seemed to feel less well-off financially over the time span of the study, while the women felt their economic circumstances had stayed about the same. The subjects, especially the women, seemed for the most part to be active and involved in community and family affairs. Almost all were satisfied with what they had accomplished in life.

On our measures of personality and adjustment, almost all the subjects' average scores were less at the 1965 assessment than at the 1956 assessment. (The TAT was an exception for both men and women, and the Opinion Conformity Scale was an exception for men.) The intermediate point of 1962 varied upward and downward over the measures. Inter-year correlations showed greater consistency on the activity-oriented measures (Activity and Attitude Inventories, Judge's Rating, and Interviewer's Rating), somewhat more so for men than for women. The Community Rating was quite consistent over the years.

To measure *individual* change we used a Longitudinal Trend Score (LTS), which was the correlation between the three years of assessment as one variable and the scores on a measure for those years as the other. Distributions of the LTS's showed that, on six of eight measures, larger proportions of women had markedly negative LTS's than markedly positive ones; this was true for men on four of eight measures. On the Mean LTS, 78 percent of the men had negative averages, indicating average downward trends, while 21 percent had positive average LTS's; their average Mean LTS was −.20. For women, 81 percent had negative Mean LTS's and 19 percent had positive average LTS's; their average Mean LTS was −.25.

When we tried to locate statistically what factors were associated with positive or negative change in the various measures, our efforts showed that, on a variety of background variables, the positive-change people could seldom be distinguished from the negative-change people.

We turned to individual case studies to show the variability in the patterns of continuity and change. We believe that these examples show that both change and continuity existed within the individuals studied, and that the influence of factors such as we investigated was often indirect and not unidirectional. We posited some reasons for this view and shall discuss them shortly.

Aging and Survival

Our second objective was to study the problem of survivorship. Our hypothesis was that survival is related to personal and social behavior, as well as to change in behavior (Chapter 4). The attrition rate of our 205 subjects, all 65 or older in 1955, was shown by a loss through death from 1955 to 1956 of 8 percent; to 1962, 44 percent; to 1965, 57 percent; to 1967, 62 percent; to 1969, 67 percent; and to 1971, 78 percent. An additional percentage, approximately 10 at the later points in time, had moved away. Potential subjects for a third-round follow-up in 1965, those living and residing in the area, totaled just 34 percent of the original subjects listed ten years earlier.

Using our 1955 baseline data, we contrasted the survivors (those living and in the area) with those known to have died. These statistical comparisons indicate the obvious relevance of chronological age as a factor in survival (younger subjects outlived the older ones) but they also show the importance of social status, as is seen in occupation of the family wage earner (higher-status persons outlived lower-status ones). Women outlived men only at one of the points in the analysis.

When we compared surviving 1956 interviewees with nonsurviving ones at successive points in time, the data showed significant differences for *women* according to age (younger ones survived better), social status (women from families with a higher-status wage earner survived more frequently), and health status (those who rated their health good or excellent in 1956 outlived those who felt their health was not so good). Sex was not a factor distinguishing survivors from nonsurvivors.

On our measures of personality and adjustment, no significant differences occurred on survival for men. For women, the measures reflecting activity—the Activity Inventory, the Attitude Inventory, and the Judge's Rating—showed survivors to be the more active, involved, and satisfied women.

We also questioned whether change in our measures was predictive of death or survival. Here we used the Longitudinal Trend Scores and compared those who died with those who continued to live—in 1967, in 1969, and in 1971. These analyses must be viewed cautiously, we said, because the number of survivors for these comparisons is very small. At all three of these points, no pattern of differences was clear. Our hypothesis that those who died had changed for the worse more often than those who continued to live was not confirmed. Also, scores on the WAIS Similarities Test given in 1965 were not predictive of survival or death.

Older People in a Small Community

To determine the attitudinal milieu in which our subjects lived, we studied the social norms or expectations that residents of Pennsboro and Green Township had for older people. We also learned how some of our subjects were reputed to behave in the community. We obtained peer-group evaluations for a sample of subjects in terms of their personality and adjustment. These data, together with our general observations, helped us to put together some impressions of the kind of place the small rural community we studied was as a place to live and age.

Social Norms: Interviews with adult respondents in the community supplied us with normative data pertaining to expectations regarding older persons' work, retirement, living arrangements, family relationships, participation in the community, and solution of their personal problems. Work and activity in general were valued, especially by the higher-status respondents. To quit work and go on public assistance when one could still work was seen as a bad thing to do. Part-time work as a means of keeping occupied was condoned. Participation in community affairs was thought to be good, but more for the benefit of the older person than for any help he could give to others. As for the interaction of adult generations in a family, it was generally felt that it was up to the adult children to decide whether or not to accept, or even listen to, their elders' advice, and that other kinds of association would be at the option of both generations of the family. The elderly should make their own decisions about remarriage, and should also decide how much they wished to be with their grandchildren. In the main, the older person was felt to be responsible fully only for himself unless his grown children were handicapped or needy in some way.

The stress on independence and responsibility for oneself was shown, too, in norms about ways to solve personal problems in old age. A person was expected to seek professional assistance himself if he needed it, or to hire household help if he could not manage alone, although some young and better-educated respondents held this view more often that did the older people themselves. The elderly were more likely to be aware that some problems were just natural to aging and that those individuals who had them would simply have to cope as best they could. Besides, outside "solutions" cost money, which was often not available.

Reputations: In our 1955 community-wide survey we asked respondents to name individuals who they felt were doing particularly well or who were not getting along well in their old age (Chapter 5). About seven of every ten of the subjects were named, and nearly half of these were referred to in a positive fashion. How positive or negative their reputations were was not related importantly to any background variables nor to our other measures of personality and adjustment. The Reputation Rating did not differentiate individuals whose personality-adjustment measures changed over the years, nor did it distinguish between survivors and nonsurvivors.

Peer-Group Evaluations: How closely do results from commonly used personality assessment procedures correspond to those derived from peers who saw persons function in the daily life of the community? To help us answer this question we worked out a method for use with selected community members who evaluated a sample of our older subjects whom they knew. We used a forced-choice, Q-sort scheme. This methodology was described in Chapter 5, where it was shown that community panelists agreed fairly well with judges who rated interview material and quite well with the evaluations by the TAT. (We viewed the latter finding with some skepticism, as we said earlier.) Reputation Ratings and the Community Rating agreed to a fair extent, too. We believe that for the most part our other procedures assessed behavior that was rather different from that commonly seen by residents of Pennsboro and Green Township.

The Q-subjects were obviously a select group, drawn as they were as the most well-known of our study population; their survival rates exceeded those of the others. Still, the Community Rating was not the differentiating variable. Data on change in Community Rating in relation to survival showed consistent differences in favor of those who continued living, but the numbers were very small.

DISCUSSION AND IMPLICATIONS

The Issues

The issue of stability and continuity versus change in personality, an issue posed by the present research, seems to us to be of more than passing importance.[3] How one views this issue deeply affects the views one holds concerning man's nature and, therefore, how one perceives most issues in a psychology of personality. It is a widely accepted assumption that a person gradually forms a characteristic personality which becomes highly resistant to change with the passage of time. Hardly anyone would disagree with the commonsense notion that there is stability and continuity over time in personality development (Kagan, 1969; Bloom, 1964), and presumably this applies to adults, including the aged, so long as they are well and free from debilitating mental illness. Nevertheless, it is recognized that the aged are a select group; the older they are the more select they are.

Indeed, it is remarkable how most people search for (and generally find) some unifying continuity and consistency, some stability in their day-to-day lives. Even behavior which is various

---

[3] As the final draft of this chapter was being written, a provocative work important to this theme became available: L. R. Goulet and P. B. Baltes (Eds.), *Life-Span Developmental Psychology: Research and Theory.* New York: Academic Press, 1970.

and discrepant is placed in some kind of unifying context of time. Mischel (1969) stated this view as follows:

> In my appraisal, the overall evidence [concerning continuity] from many sources [clinical, experimental, developmental, correlational] shows the human mind to function like an extraordinarily effective reducing valve that creates and maintains the perception of continuity even in the face of perpetual observed changes in actual behavior. Often this cognitive construction of continuity, while not arbitrary, is only very tenuously related to the phenomena that are construed (p. 1012).

Thus, Mischel indicated that, even in the face of real discontinuity, personal constructs about ourselves and others ("both in our roles as persons and as psychologists") are often "extremely stable and highly resistant to change" (p. 1012), a point raised by Kelly (1955, p. 659), as was mentioned previously.

The Search for Regularity

It is not surprising either that scientific researchers who seek out processes, laws, and predictions that are common to all persons tend to emphasize aspects of stability, continuity, and orderliness at the expense of objectively viewing variation and change in human personality. Statistical manipulation has helped scientists in their search. The scales often seem to be tipped in favor of *continuity*, provided statistical significance is reached, even though only a tiny portion of the variance may be accounted for. A corollary to this bias is that the social scientist usually looks at group data that reveal support for general laws and predictions; less often does he attend to individual patterns that show variation.

Measured Consistency

In addition, as scientists we have concentrated upon those characteristics of the personality or behavior which could be measured by current techniques. These methods are probably quite well suited to the study of malfunctioning, the sensory processes, and even animal behavior; their use has yielded stable and consistent patterns of behavior. Bloom, for example, in speaking of *human* characteristics, limited himself to those characteristics which can be represented quantitatively and on a single scale. He pointed out:

> It is clear that there are many characteristics which can be better described by the use of qualities and descriptions rather than through the use of quantities. We have *not* included such characteristics in this work—not because we regard them as unstable, but because we have used data analysis techniques which are more appropriate for characteristics which can be represented quantitatively (1964, p. 206; emphasis added).

Furthermore, in attempting to be precise and accurate in measurements, behavioral scientists have often ignored the great complexity, diversity, and variability of behavior. Moreover, the complexity and variation in environments have often been ignored. Generally, behavioral phenomena have been reduced to a few simple limits. Kuo (1967) provided an apt example:

> . . . the behavior of a fly would be a very complicated affair if we took into account the complexity, variability, and interplay of such determining factors as morphology, biophysics, biochemistry, developmental history, environmental context and the various characteristics of the stimulating objects. However, if we simply put a fly in a very small blackened box with two small openings both penetrated by outside light and send a stream of cold air through one opening and a stream of warm air through the other, we could predict with almost mathematical accuracy by which of the two openings the fly would escape from the box and in how many trials. But, in so doing, we must ignore other details of the fly's activities inside the black box. In other words, the success of such an experimental prediction is due not to the accuracy of mathematical theories or models, but rather to the oversimplification of the experimental situation in animal learning (p. 7).

Consistency in Personality

In connection with the question of continuity versus change in personality over time, the literature shows that the strongest evidence in support of stability and continuity comes in the intellective or cognitive dimensions of personality. Although research into these dimensions has been confined for the most part to children and adolescents, studies in the development of cognitive style point impressively to developmental continuity (Kagan, 1969; Witkin, Goodenough, Karp, 1967). The curves compiled by Bloom (1964) concerning the growth of intelligence also present an attractive argument for the notion of stability and continuity over time. Strong's study of interests over a period of 22 years also suggests consistency with time (Strong, 1951).

However, when the dimensions of interpersonal or social behavior of personality are examined, the evidence for stability over time, especially from adolescence into the adult years or across time within adulthood, is inconclusive.

Several recent reports have failed to show predictability from childhood to adulthood in the area of social interaction. In a review of data concerning school achievement and future job success, the Harvard team of Kohlberg and Mayer (1971) reported that high school dropouts apparently did as well as high school graduates who did not attend college and that college graduates with poor grades do as well as those with high grades. In addition, they found, on the basis of longitudinal research, no evidence that such characteristics as self-confidence, spontaneity, curiosity, and self-discipline in preschool children have any predictive value for adult life-adjustment. In a study of deviant children grown up, Robins (1966) showed that while antisocial behavior in childhood was predictive of sociopathic behavior in adults, children's withdrawn personality characteristics were not associated with later adult pathology of any kind. In a follow-up study of the attainments of the mentally retarded at middle life, Baller (1967) showed low predictability of adult behavior from childhood: a group of persons with I.Q.'s in childhood of less than 70 actually managed considerably better as adults than had been predicted. A study by Maas (1963) of 20 adults, who as children had been separated from their parents during World War II in England and then returned to their parents, found no serious psychological disturbance in this group. All of these adults were functioning well. Bowlby et al. (1956) found great variation in personality outcomes in a follow-up study of 60 children who had been in a sanitarium for tuberculosis for varying periods of time before their fourth birthdays.

From the studies dealing with continuity in specific personality traits over the span of years from middle childhood or early adolescence to adulthood (Anderson, 1959, 1960; Beilin, 1957; Cantoni, 1955; Hertz and Baker, 1951; Jayaswal and Stott, 1955), no definite conclusions emerged; some modest associations were found in some traits, marked changes in others. Reports from the California Adolescent Study of the relationship between personality characteristics rated during adolescence and similar characteristics measured in adulthood demonstrated consistency in some and inconsistency in others. Based on analysis of data from this Berkeley study, Harold Jones et al. (1958) concluded that adolescent ratings of drives are often associated with adolescent maladjustment, but that they are not highly predictive of adult maladjustment.

Certainly, part of the problem lies in defining what constitutes personality, not to mention what operations one uses to describe it. Also, developmental psychologists who have concentrated their efforts on studies of children growing up are inclined to view adulthood as a period of steadiness, certainly as compared to childhood. We would prefer that this point be qualified by the idea of *relative stability*, but that this should *not* preclude the possibility of change.

Other longitudinal research is instructive in this context. Symonds and Jensen (1961) conducted a thirteen-year follow-up study of 28 young men and women who were among 40 whom Symonds had originally seen as adolescents (1949). In studying their expressions of fantasy, the authors reported "a marked persistence of themes," but changes as well:

> There are general changes in the thematic content of the stories over the thirteen-year interval. . . . All of our evidence points to a lessening of the stormy, violent factors of adolescence expressed in stories of adventure and excitement containing much hostile aggression and romance; in their place are much less exciting and more matter-of-fact

stories tinged with depression. . . . In many instances it was clear that adolescent fantasy has worked itself out into open expression in behavior and/or personality in later years (Symonds and Jensen, 1961, p. 209).

Further, these authors hypothesized that "change in fantasy is a function of change in environment; if the situation does not change, in general, the fantasies do not change" (p. 210). They concluded:

There is a high degree of consistency in overt personality characteristics over the thirteen-year interval in (a) physical characteristics; (b) general personality characteristics, including aggressiveness. . . ; (c) nervous signs; (d) hobbies; and (e) attitudes (Symonds and Jensen, 1961, p. 210).

In a follow-up investigation of River City (Havighurst, Bowman, Liddle, Matthews, and Pierce, 1962) boys and girls at about age 23, Davis (1971) attempted to determine combinations of certain antecedent variables, measured in childhood and adolescence, which were predictive of "Life Satisfaction," "Work Satisfaction," and "Social Mobility" in young adults. She found that findings differed for males and females: for all three consequent variables, predictions could be made more successfully for women than for men. The antecedent variable of "Initial Adult Status" (measured most closely in time to the later follow-up interviews) was most predictive for females' Life Satisfaction, suggesting more continuity for them than for the males. For males, the variable most predictive of Life Satisfaction, but still accounting for rather little of the variance, was "Aggressive Maladjustment." Life satisfaction, measured by an adaptation, for young adults, of a scale devised for older ones (Neugarten, Havighurst, and Tobin, 1961), constituted a kind of global personal-social adjustment measure and could, Davis found, be predicted better than the other consequent variables. Thus Davis' analysis found some continuity but also change from childhood to early adulthood. Both change and continuity occurred also within the population studied by Oppenheimer and Wood (1966, 1967a, 1967b).

Frustrations and Difficulties

In reporting "a study of the natural growth of personality," White (1966) presented and analyzed in detail three individuals' "lives in progress" throughout young adulthood. One paragraph of his expresses the kinds of difficulties our own research problem has faced:

> Although our insight has been greatly benefited by a combined social, biological, and psychodynamic approach, we have also experienced certain enduring frustrations. It has bothered us that general concepts such as social class and occupation, drive and motive, psychosexual stage and parental attitude, have required so many qualifications in order to fit the individual case. We have repeatedly found that general concepts did not help us to understand process or change, which always had to be described with reference to many particulars. It has also been confusing to realize that so many forces operate at once in a given personality, producing an elaborate system of interconnected events rather than a simple model of cause and effect. But perhaps our most recurrent difficulty has been that of accounting for natural growth. It seemed easier to explain the more rigid, crippled, and irrational features of our subjects' personalities than to understand the constructive side of their development. Clearly we must devote more attention to what happens when lives are in progress (1966, p. 366; author's emphasis omitted).

White followed this statement with a discussion of some of the ambiguities of the concepts of mental health and adjustment, and then delineated five "growth trends" indicating both the *process* of change and a *direction* of change: (1) the stabilizing of ego identity, (2) the freeing of personal relationships, (3) the deepening of interests, (4) the humanizing of values, and (5) the expansion of caring. However, White continued:

> Growth in a given direction takes place under certain conditions and through certain types of experience. It is not just something that happens because we grow older. If in addition to designating trends we can identify the crucial conditions under which development occurs, we

shall be taking a definite step forward in the understanding of natural growth (White, 1966, pp. 373-374).

It seems rather clear that no simple conclusions about consistency of personality, especially with reference to the adult years, are possible from existing research. There is evidence of continuity, and there are also data pointing to change over time.

Explanations for Discontinuity

In the face of evidence of change and discontinuity in personality, two explanations have been widely offered. One pertains to the imperfections and grossness of measurement of the tools and tests, as well as to other methodological problems. (This type of "unreliability" is said to account for differences in the Sears, Maccoby, and Levin replication study of Yarrow, Campbell, and Burton [1968].) We are well aware of these problems and acknowledge that our own measurement methodology has several serious limitations. Kuo (1967, p. 19) reminded us: "It is a dangerous procedure to arrive at any scientific generalizations from naturalistic observations, especially when such observations are of short duration, because the observer may not have seen enough of the variability of behavior and environment in the field." What is more, *experimental* methods of investigating human behavior severely limit the variables that can be studied as well as the ways in which they can be controlled.

Bloom (1964 pp. 10, 221) also admonished social scientists to develop more precise measures *of the environment;* we would add: of *changes* in the environment (Copp, 1965). The present research actually assumed stability in the environment when concern was directed toward natural changes within the individual. In our interpretation, however, we have implied that our initial assumption that our study community would not and did not change was naive. While Pennsboro and Green Township probably changed less markedly than many communities, important social changes have occurred and are occurring there. We believe in the necessity to measure such change.

We are more and more of the opinion, however, that the inconsistencies and discontinuities found in our own subjects and in others, especially those involving the social dimensions of personality, reflect the way persons *are*. They are not simply reflections of problems of measurement. In the drive to find laws of behavior, scientists tend to perceive only behavioral regularities and stereotypes, neglecting to see new forms and expressions of behavior. We do not mean to suggest that there are no unifying laws of nature—we only propose that personality consistencies are often more *forced* than real and that change in many of the dimensions of personality *is* a state of nature.

A second argument for continuity of personality in the face of variation over time is commonly discussed in terms of the genotypic-phenotypic characteristcs. Hartman, Kris, and Lowenstein (1946, p. 19) stated it succinctly:

> We assume that the essential elements in the structure of personality exist in children of our civilization at the age of five or six. Developmental processes occurring after that age can be described as modifications, as enrichment, or in pathological cases, as restriction of the then existing structure.

Bloom also expressed the genotypic-phenotypic argument in his discussion of the attributes of stable characteristics:

> Thus general intelligence or general academic achievement must be manifestations of fundamental properties of the central nervous system as well as of an underlying pattern of basic habits, attitudes and ways of relating to the world. . . . We would distinguish the underlying structure or pattern from the mode of expressing it. Thus aggressiveness may arise from an underlying personality make-up, but it may be expressed in many different ways. . . . Closely related to this is the idea that a characteristic may be very stable although the expression of it may constantly change (1964, p. 208).

While the genotypic-phenotypic argument seems to be shared widely among personality theorists, we believe it does not adequately explain change or variation in behavior. Indeed, it merely tends to diminish the possibility of seeing important, dynamic new behaviors (Becker, 1964). It may not be tidy or convenient for a scientist to see human behavior as encompassing great diversity and variation, but the possibility that this is indeed true of nature must be admitted. To accept the possibility, for example, that a man was once a hostile, egocentric person but now *is* indeed a warm and loving one is to accept the possibility of *real* change and not simply of "an overtly more acceptable way of dealing with people through mechanisms of defense." The genotypic-phenotypic explanation of change in personality is much too simple to account for complex behavior, especially for behavior for which unilinear causes appear fragile at best.

Maccoby's concept of "branching" expressions of a particular characteristic (1969) offers a useful concept of combining the *essential continuity* of personality, but more important for the issue at hand is her notion of the dropping off of some characteristics. Speaking of children, Maccoby hypothesized that they "not only mature at different rates, but that they mature in different directions" (1969, pp. 10-11). She suggested that with time "individuals become progressively more different from each other at the same time that all are becoming more complex, and while all are still maintaining the hallmarks of their earlier levels of individuality." Further: "We must recognize the possibility that if such differentiation occurs, one branch may continue to grow and subdivide further, while another branch remains static or even withers" (p. 11). A serious weakness in this concept of tree-like growth of personality, she said, is the implication that the separate branches develop independently of one another. "This is clearly not the case," she said. "Behavioral 'systems' interact. . . . Ultimately, we must find ways of describing the organizations and reorganizations that occur at successive stages" (pp. 12-13).

Generally speaking, practitioners working in human service professions have not had much faith in stimulating change or in modifying behavior in important ways among older adults—even those past 45 or 50. The popular ideology seems to be that indeed "you can't teach an old dog new tricks" and that this certainly applies to personality as well as to skills. This folkway (if it be that) does contribute to our unwillingness to see change or to work to effect change in important behavior.

Naturalness of Change

Actually, it should not be difficult for the social scientist who believes in an active, dynamic organism to accept the notion that change and lack of consistency in personality are pragmatically valid. Three concepts make this possible.

1. The great variation in the makeup of any individual human being, growing from the intricate and complex interrelationships of his genetic structure, his changing physiology, and his developmental history. These are never static. While it is true that structure limits possibilities for behavior, it is also true that a given individual never exploits the myriad of behavioral possibilities open to him by his structure.   •

2. The ever-changing environmental context with which the individual interacts. Recent experimental research in behavior modification (Bandura, 1969; Bijou, 1965, 1970) has demonstrated the dependency of behavior upon conditions, a point also made by Lawton (1970). In a study such as the present one, placed in a "natural" setting rather than in a contrived or experimental one where "controls" would be in force, it might be expected that an individual would change in the face of changes in his relationships with significant other people as well as with the larger community and with the physical environment. This is possible, we think, in spite of our having explicitly chosen a "relatively stable" community. We would question, in the context of personality interaction, whether any socially inhabited environment is ever stable!

3. The great potentiality of the human, especially of the normal adult human, to monitor and to determine much of his own behavior. We believe he can and does act and react, evaluate and reevaluate, to regulate and control much of his overt behavior and his attitudes and beliefs—all in the light of his developmental history and of his perceptions of the future. This is to say that the normal adult holds executive abilities that give him *relative power, within limits,* to determine features of his own personality and other behavior. The possibility of his constructive (and "reconstructive") use of such "person power" in "becoming" (Allport, 1955) what he wants is too seldom recognized.

This view of man assumes his potential for higher intellective activity (and the adaptive and survival value of such functioning) in much the same way that Piaget has credited the late- and postadolescent with cognitive abilities that enable him to "take his own thought as an object and reason about it" (Elkind, 1968, p.

141). This would include his ability to think abstractly about himself and to hypothesize about his own future.

The adult's potential power to organize and reorganize for himself such determinants of personality as roles and situations, group memberships, and even constitutional determinants (Chapter 1) presumes that man does not simply act out a predestined, preprogrammed life pattern. However, we are not required to discard the notion that a number of characteristics or features of personality are predetermined or that history and social and cultural and economic circumstances are determined by forces external to the individual himself. We agree with Gordon Allport's statement, "Personality is less a finished product than a transitive process. While it has some stable features, it is at the same time continually undergoing change" (1955, p. 19).

Our main concern, of course, was with consistency or change in later maturity and old age. We found more subjects changing for the worse than changing for the better or remaining the same on our measures. But change they did. Perhaps it was surprising that more of our subjects had not declined in this late period in adulthood, especially since they were living in a natural environment in which no special efforts were being made to promote positive change.

Our search for factors that were associated with such change has not met with much success. It appears that events or factors *per se*, such as those we studied, are "filtered" through the individual's own personality system to enable him to see them in his own unique, satisfying, and sometimes *new* ways.

Perhaps observers should say that this *is* nature and discontinue the search for understanding certain regularities and stable aspects of man's behavior. However, we believe that questions must continue to be asked and answers continue to be sought! We suggest that researchers ask not *whether* adults can change but, rather, under what circumstances they *can* and *do* change. And when we say *adults*, we explicitly include the aged.

In formulating hypotheses about human behavioral change in adulthood, we need, of course, to build into them important, changing environmental variables and to include, we think, the concept of the criticalness of certain periods in individuals' lives. Bloom proposed that "a characteristic can be more drastically affected by the environment in its most rapid period of growth than in its least rapid period of growth" (1964, p. 210). We would posit that *the environment affects personal and social characteristics in adults during their most rapid period of decline or during periods of transition in either the individual or his life situation, when (1) the circumstances are most ambiguous, either in outward reality or as personally perceived; (2) when competency is in question, by self or others; and (3) when expectations of self and others are most unclear.*

This proposition emphasizes the essential relationship between environmental circumstances and personal abilities and perceptions, and shows them as interacting and as having outcomes that may be changes in old behaviors or even new and emergent behaviors. Such outcomes are possible not because of genetic factors but also because of developmental history, experience, and the cognitive capabilities of the adult to monitor, analyze, synthesize, hypothesize, and to make use of environmental inputs in unique ways.

Personality and Society

In a simple, highly stable, agrarian society it might be argued that the development of a particular personal-social characteristic might be identified and operationally defined, and that environmental forces might be put into motion to assure the development of that characteristic in the population. The responsibility of the society in such a case would be relatively simple and clear-cut.

The ever-changing character of modern life and the highly complex nature of human relations and interactions within our society and with others make it essential that our society begin to cope with the difficult yet inescapable questions of how to assist its members not only to adapt but to realize their potential as creators and givers of meaning to society. This places a heavy responsibility on individuals to define for themselves (and with and for others who matter to them) what their potential is and what their optimal development could be. That such definitions and their manifestations will be diverse, certainly not uniform in quality, could be expected, but we are persuaded that our society will function the better for this freedom and responsibility. This view is in harmony with the philosophy that basic human needs are cared for within an optimal societal system through provision of diverse opportunities for individual fulfillment based upon individual choice.

Value on Individuality

There is a further point that should be emphasized in this connection: In a society in which individuality is respected and encouraged, in which social policy is determined by the benefit to individuals, there can be no room for using a criterion of chronological age as determining who should be served. The fact that the future is of shorter duration for one who is old than for one who is young should not determine the choice. Clearly there should be enough services and goods for both. Society should be enabled to provide the best possible opportunities so that all its citizens can meet their goals and serve their aspirations.

A desirable goal for our society, then, is to *increase* the range of acceptable individual behaviors. Work done with lower animals suggests that the wider the range and variety of the environment, the wider the range of individual behavioral responses and the more flexible the individual (Burghardt and Hess, 1966; Harlow et al., 1965). We would expect that older adults who live within—and experience—a supportive environment that nourishes social and psychological diversity for individuals, families, and organizations and institutions would have a greater range of behaviors for their use in organizing and reorganizing their behavior to meet the requirements of a changing environment. We believe they would be less inclined toward personality disturbance and disintegration, or toward abnormal or antisocial behavior. Theoretically such older persons could more easily alter their environments or choose among environments that can best serve their needs.

Later Adulthood and Growth Potential

The latter period of adult life is, like earlier ones, a time of change and transition. It is often characterized by physical decline and a decrease in energy, but it also can be a time of psychological growth. During this period, attitudes, aspirations, and one's concept of self are sensitive and vulnerable to many stimuli (Lawton, 1970); they are subject to both dramatic and subtle changes that are crucial in shaping the remaining years of the individual's life. Decisions are made or deferred, actions are taken or rejected, and the effects of these decisions and actions can be deep and significant.

It is at these points of personal choice, when motivation is high for change toward new behaviors, that the society can provide an environment which encourages the older person's potential to be flexible. Such an environment would not capitalize upon such turning points to adapt the individual to *its* goals, but recognize them as points of personal growth for the older adult himself. We must increase our sensitivity and responsiveness to such possibilities for growth in late periods of adulthood as well as during earlier stages of life.

It seems quite imprudent to speak of a *single*, optimum environment for all people. Rather, we prefer a society that strives to provide a variety of behavioral settings which offer continued opportunities for individually satisfying involvement, for the possibility of new and stimulating experiences, and for varieties of behaviors which can be freely chosen. Recognition that growth and change in persons *of all ages* and characteristics may be possible is essential to a truly humanitarian and democratic society.

APPENDICES

Appendix A
Press Release, 1965

THE PENNSYLVANIA STATE UNIVERSITY
Department of Public Information
312 Old Main Bldg., University Park, Pa. 16802
Phone, 814-865-7517

NEWS

University Park, Pa., May 27, 1965. A study to determine what happens to people as they grow older will be continued in Liberty County, Pennsylvania, during the next few weeks, Joseph H. Britton, in charge of the Study of Adulthood, The Pennsylvania State University, said today.

In 1956 and in 1962 interviewers talked with residents 65 years of age and older who were living in Pennsboro and Green Township, Liberty County. Interviewers again will ask the cooperation of those residents, seeking information on activities they assume, and what changes are made in community and family life during the later years.

"We particularly want to learn how people adapt to the changes which the years bring," Mr. Britton said.

Those who will do the interviewing are Mrs. Jean O. Britton, Mrs. Ruth Hummel, Mrs. Joy Olson, David H. Olson, and Mark L. Knapp, all of State College, Pennsylvania.

Expressing his appreciation for the "fine cooperation we have had from Liberty County residents in the past," Mr. Britton reported that his previous studies have shown that most residents "get along well, even when faced with serious health problems."

"Our studies will not be finished, however, until we follow these people as they age," he added. "We want to learn how they live now, how they use their time, and what they think of things these days."

He said that the information being collected will contribute importantly to knowledge of how to improve the well-being of older citizens throughout the country.

Appendix B
1955 Information Sheet

The Pennsylvania State University

1955 Information Sheet   Confidential   Schedule No._____
                                                 Interviewer_____
                                                 Informant_____

Name of person interviewed_____
Address_____
Own or rent house_____
House Type_____
Area lived in_____
Information on household occupants:

	NAME	RELATIONSHIP TO INTERVIEWER	AGE	LAST GRADE OF SCHOOL COMPLETED	OCCUPATION (EXPLAIN)
1.					
2.					
3.					
4.					
5.					
6.					
7.					
8.					
9.					
10.					
11.					
12.					

Interviewer's rating:

_____Very cooperative

_____Cooperative   Comments

_____Indifferent

_____Uncooperative

_____Definitely uncooperative

Appendix C
1955 Interview Schedule

The Pennsylvania State University
Committee for the Study of Adulthood

1955 Interview Schedule   1955 Schedule No._____
                                       Section No._____House No._____
                    Confidential   Interviewer_____
                                       Informant_____
                                       Date_____

The purpose of this study is to gather information which will contribute to a
better understanding of problems of older people and how to meet them

One of the problems is when to retire

1. When do you think a person should retire?

Now I'm going to suggest to you things which people 65 or older sometimes do. Some
of these are good, others are not so good. Tell me how you feel about them. Remember
there are no right and wrong answers and your replies are completely confidential.
We want to know what you think about older people doing these things.

2. Bill Brown was in good health. But, since he had saved enough money to retire,
    he sold out to his son, and he and his wife moved away.

3. A man I know stopped working, but decided to stay around to advise his son.

4. Tom Smith found full time work too big a job. He turned things over to some-
    one else and now works a little when things get rushed.

5. Then there was Sam. He could have continued working, but by the time he was
    66, he felt that he needed a rest, so he quit and applied for public assistance.

6. Do you know some older person around here who is getting along well in his
    retirement?

    Anyone else?

7. Is there some older person who is not getting along so well in retirement?

Older people often have to adjust their living arrangements. A lower income, death
of a husband or wife, and poor health sometimes make these changes necessary.

8. What do you think are the best living arrangements for an older person?

9. Mr. Everett is too feeble to care for himself, so he wants to live in an
    old people's home rather than move in with his married daughter.

10. Because she is pretty lonesome after the death of her husband, Mrs. Sayles
    rented out her own home and moved in with her married daughter.

11. Do you know some older person around here who has good living arrangements?

12. Do you know some older person who has not made such good arrangements?

It's important for families to understand each other and get along with each other.
Here are some things older people and their families do. Tell me how you feel
about the way these people live.

13. When Beth's husband died he left her fairly well off. But, rather than spend
    the money, she lives as cheaply as possible so she can pass it on to her
    children.

14. Mr. and Mrs. Green know lots about how things should be run. They were always good managers. Now they give plenty of good advice to their married children.

15. Mrs. Cutler insists that her married children spend all the holidays at her house. She likes to have the whole family together at these times.

16. An older person who is widowed is often lonesome. What do you think about marriage for such a person?

17. Mrs. Black doesn't care to be with her grandchildren. She had her fill of children when she brought up her own.

18. Do you know some older person around here who gets along well with his family?

19. Do you know some older person who doesn't get along so well?

Sometimes life is pretty hard for an older person and he needs help. I'm going to mention some of the problems old folks have. Please tell what you think they ought to do about them.

20. An older person with no family in town is often lonesome, and would like some-one to talk things over with. What should this person do?

21. Mrs. Cook hardly knows where to turn. Her mother who is over 80 has been acting queer and the whole family is upset.

22. Bill Jenkins hasn't felt well for a long time. He has all kinds of aches and thinks that he has a really serious disease. He wants to know where to go.

23. Life has not been easy for Mr. and Mrs. Rogers. Now they have really had hard luck and are almost out of money.

24. Emily lives alone. Although her hands are swollen she manages most things pretty well. The heavier housekeeping jobs, however, are practically impossible for her.

We've talked about several problems about getting help.

25. Do you know some older person around here who is bothered by any of these things?

26. Do you know some older person who doesn't seem to be bothered by any of these things?

It's important for old folks to have friends and be happy in the community.

27. Do you think older people should get into things or stay out of them?

Please tell how you feel about what these old folks did.

28. Jim Murray would like to join some community clubs. He is in good health and has some time on his hands. Which groups around here would be glad to have an older member?

29. A person 65 retired from work and dropped out of all the old activities.

30. Mrs. Rand is 67 and has lots of ideas. She likes people and would make a good leader. Which groups are suited to have an older person as an officer or leader?

31. John Martin is assistant fire chief; he's careful never to express an idea which the younger firemen will not like.

32. An older person I know likes to be with and work with younger people most of the time. What do you think about this?

33. Do you know some older person around here who fits into things nicely?

34. Do you know some older person around here who doesn't fit in so well?

35. Do you think of any other problems older people have that we haven't discussed?

36. Is there another family living here (in this house)?

Appendix D
1956 Interview Schedule

The Pennsylvania State University
Committee for Study of Adulthood

1956 Interview Schedule

Confidential

1956 Schedule No._____
1955 Schedule No._____
Interviewer_____
Date_____
Checked by_____

The purpose of this study is to gather information which will help build understanding that may better the life conditions of middle-aged and older persons. I have a number of questions I'll ask, and if you think of additional things we need to think about, add them as we go along.

1. Are you a man?   or a woman?

2. How old were you on your last birthday?

3. In what country were you born?

4. In what country was your father born?

5. Your mother?

6. What was the last grade of school that you finished?

7. If you went to an ungraded school, what was your age when you left school?

Now I want to ask you about your health.

8. How would you rate your health at the present time?
   --very poor, poor, fair, good, excellent?

9. Is your health better or worse now than it was when you were 55 years of age?
   --worse now, about the same, better now?

10. What are your serious physical problems?
    --poor sight, blind or nearly so, hard of hearing, deaf or nearly so, crippled arms, hands or legs, general rheumatic stiffness, heart trouble, stomach trouble, high blood pressure, no physical problems, other (what is it?)?

11. Here is a list of difficulties that people often have. If any of these bother you, please tell me.
    --shortness of breath at night, shortness of breath after slight exercise, heart burn, swelling of feet or legs, feeling tired, have had nervous breakdown, difficulty in urination, constipation, aching joints, backache, gas pains, belching, headaches, none of these difficulties.

12. How many days did you spend sick in bed last year?
    --all the time, a month or more, two to four weeks, a few days, none.

13. Which of the following things often trouble you?
    --sleeplessness, bad dreams, tire too easily, food doesn't taste good, feel "blue", nervousness, dislike noise, worry about my health, forgetfulness, troubled with none of these.

14. Have you had any serious accidents in the last five years?

    --yes, no.

178

Directions for   1956 Schedule No._____
  Thematic Apperception Test   Interviewer_____
                                        Date_____

<u>Now this is where we want you to use your imagination.</u>

<u>I have some pictures here</u> (Hold up cards without revealing the picture sides.) <u>and I'm going to show them to you one at a time.</u>

<u>I'd like you to look at the picture, think about it for a moment, and then say what you think is going on in the picture. Just make up a story about it. Whatever you say will be all right. You can make up any kind of story you want to. Don't forget, use your imagination.</u>

<u>Here's the first picture.</u> (Expose card No. 7 and hand it to the older person.)

(Wait for a response, record it below, and continue to wait and record until the story has been completed or until you judge that the older person needs prodding to finish the task.)

What are the people doing in that picture? What's happening?

What is the older man thinking about?

What is the younger man thinking about?

How does the older man feel?

How does the younger man feel?

What happened before this?

How will it all turn out in the end?

(Commend the older person for his effort in an appropriate manner with a comment like "you did all right on that one, now let's try another one" or "that was very good; here's another picture, let's try another story.") (Expose card no. 6 and hand it to the older person.)

<u>Now use your imagination and make up any kind of story you want to.</u> (Wait for a response, record it below, and continue to wait until you judge that the older person requires prodding.)

What are the people doing in that picture? What's happening?

What is the woman thinking about?

What is the man thinking about

How does the woman feel?

How does the man feel?

What happened before this?

How will it all turn out in the end?

(Again commend the older person with an appropriate comment, ending with, "now here's the last picture, how about making up another story. Use your imagination and say whatever you want to.")

(Expose card no. 10 and hand it to the older person. Wait for a response, record it below, and continue to wait until you judge that the older person requires prodding.)

What are the people doing in that picture? What's happening?

What is the man thinking about?

What is the woman thinking about?

How does the man feel?

How does the woman feel?

What happened before this?

How will it all turn out in the end?

(Again commend the older person for his effort and express your appreciation for his cooperation.)

Now let's continue with the other questions. These are about your family.

15. Which of the following applies to you?
--never been married, married and living with husband or wife, married but separated, divorced, widow or widower (How many years ago were you widowed?)

16. How do you rate the happiness of your (last) marriage?
--very unhappy, unhappy, average, happy, very happy.

17. If you had your life to live over, would you marry the same person?
--no, possibly, certainly.

18. How many living children do you now have?

19. With whom are you living?
--with husband or wife, with husband or wife and children, with children alone, alone, with parents, with relatives, with friends, others (who are they?)

20. How often do you see some of your family or close relatives?
--less than once a year, about once a month, once or twice a week, every day, have no family or relatives.

21. If you have a family or close relatives, do they neglect you?
--yes, completely, a little, not at all.

22. If you have a family or close relatives, do they try to interfere in your affairs?
--yes, often, yes, once in a while, almost never.

Would you give me your opinion on these questions?

*23. Do you think an older widow should live alone rather than move in with one of her grown children?

--yes, no, with qualifications (W/Q).

*24. Should parents expect their grown children to come home on holidays?
--yes, no, W/Q.

*25. Should an older person try hard to save his money in order to leave it to his children?
--yes, no, W/Q.

Now about your friends:

26. How many friends would you say you have?
--none, one to four, five to nine, ten or more.

27. How many of these are such close friends that you can talk to them about almost anything?

28. About how often do you visit with children or young people who are friends? (please include nieces, nephews, and grandchildren.)
    --less than once a year, a few times a year, once or twice a month, about once a week, every day, have no friends among children or young people.

Now about your leisure and recreation:

29. How much free time do you have?
    --all day, a half day, a few hours, almost none.

30. What do you do in your free time?
    --work in and around the house, work in garden or yard, work on some hobby, listen to the radio, watch TV, farm work, write letters, write books, articles, poems, etc., attend movies, attend theaters, lectures, concerts, attend clubs, lodges, other meetings, shop, participate in community or church work, play golf, or other sports, play cards or other table games, take rides, visit or entertain friends, sew, crochet, or knit, read, just sit and think, other (what?)

Now about clubs and organizations:

31. Here is a list of organizations. Do you now belong to any of these?
    --lodge, union, study group, charitable or welfare organization, veterans' organization, card or other social club, club for older people, business or professional group, church club or circle, women's club, P.T.A., music or art association or club, patriotic society, fire company, other (what?).

32. If you hold office, in which organization is it?

33. How many club meetings do you usually attend each month?
    --none, less than one a month, one or two a month, one a week, two or more a week.

34. Do you give more or less time to organizations now than when you were 55 years old?
    --less now, about the same, more now.

35. If you give less time now, why is it?
    --not physically able to attend meetings, not interested, can't afford it, moved to a new neighborhood or city, other (what?).

*36. Do you think belonging to a lodge, the fire company or a club would do an older person any good?
    --yes, no, W/Q.

Now about your employment:

37. During your adult life, have you earned money, either working for others or for yourself?
    --yes, no.

    (If the answer to Question 37 is
    "No," go to # 45.)

38. What work have you done most of the time during your adult years? (Tell what kind of work it was--for example, labor on a road construction gang, teller in a bank, etc.)

39. Comparing what you have done with the work of your brothers, sisters and first cousins, would you say that you have done:
    --not as well as they did, about as well as they did, better than they did.

40. Are you working now?
    --yes, full-time; yes, part-time; no.

41. If you are working what do you do?

42. If you are working now, either part-time or full-time, how does this work
    compare with what you did at the age of 55?

    Is the present amount earned: less, same, more.

    Do you enjoy your present job: less, same, more.

43. If you are not working full-time, why not?
    --can't find work, can't work because of health, retired, don't want a job,
    prefer to work part-time, married and stopped paid work.

44. If you are not working now, how long has it been since you held your last
    full-time job?   _____Years.

Tell me your opinion to these questions:

*45. Do you think an older person should retire and go on public assistance when
     he can still work?
     --yes, no, W/Q.

*46. Should a couple retire and turn their business over to their son just to
     give him a start in business?
     --yes, no, W/Q.

*47. Should a person hold on to a job just as long as he is physically able?
     --yes, no, W/Q.

*48. After he retires, should an older person take on part-time work in order to
     have something to do even if he doesn't need the money?
     --yes, no, W/Q.

*49. Even if he can't handle a part-time job, should a person who has retired try
     to find something to do just to keep busy?
     --yes, no, W/Q.

*50. If a man has retired and turned his business over to his son, should he
     try to help his son by giving him advice?
     --yes, no, W/Q.

51. How would you describe your present position in life?
    --can't make ends meet, enough to get along, comfortable, well-to-do,
    wealthy.

52. Are you in a better or worse position now than you were at age 55?
    --worse now, about the same, better now.

53. What is your chief means of support?
    --your (your husband's) present earnings, Social Security, Old Age Assistance
    from the state, pension from earlier occupation, relief agency, aid from children,
    aid from parents, payments from insurance annuities, investments or savings,
    other (what?).

54. Do you own your own home?
    --no; yes, still paying for it; yes, clear.

55. What is your religion?
    --Roman Catholic; Greek Catholic; Jewish; Protestant, Denomination_____
    Other (what?)

56. Are you a church member?
    --yes, no.

57. How often do you attend religious services?
    --never, less than once a month, once or twice a month, once a week, twice
    a week or oftener.

58. Do you believe in an after life?
    --no, not sure, yes, sure of it.

59. How often do you listen to church services over the radio or television?
    --never, once in a while, about once or twice a week, three or more times a week.

60. How often do you read the Prayer Book, Bible, or other religious book?
    --never, less than once a week, once a week, every day.

What is your opinion to these questions?

*61. Does an older person who is lonely usually get help from the minister?
    --yes, no, W/Q.

*62. When an older person acts "queer," should he be taken to the doctor?
    --yes, no, W/Q.

*63. Should the family of an older couple help if the couple is almost out of money?
    --yes, no, W/Q.

64. As you look back over your life, in general would you call it:
    --very happy, moderately happy, average, unhappy.

65. How do you feel about what you have accomplished in life?
    --well satisfied, reasonably satisfied, dissatisfied.

(Go on to the last section.)

Chicago Attitude Inventory   1956 Schedule No._____
Personal Relations (P) and   Interviewer_____
Sociability (S) Scale   Date_____

I'm going to read a series of questions to you. There really is no right or wrong answer to any of them; we'd like to know how you feel about them. We want you to answer yes or no. It'll probably be hard to make up your mind on some of these, but tell me with yes or no how you feel about the question.

1. I feel just miserable most of the time. . . . . .Y___ N___ WQ___

2. I have more friends now than I ever had before. . . . . . . .Y___ N___ WQ___

P 3. If you could have your way, would you change a lot of
      things about human nature? . . . . Y___ N___ WQ___

4. I am happy only when I have definite work to do. . . . . . . Y___ N___ WQ___

5. I am just able to make ends meet. . . . . .Y___ N___ WQ___

P 6. Do you agree with this--? Most people do their work
      even when no one is watching them. . . . . Y___ N___ WQ___

7. Religion is fairly important in my life. . . . . Y___ N___ WQ___

8. I am some use to those around me . . . . Y___ N___ WQ___

S 9. Do you enjoy getting to know people?. . . . . Y___ N___ WQ___

10. This is the dreariest time of my life . . . . Y___ N___ WQ___

11. My family likes to have me around . . . . Y___ N___ WQ___

P 12. Do you think most people are paid as much as they
       deserve for what they do?. . . . . Y___ N___ WQ___

13. I am perfectly satisfied with my health. . . . . Y___ N___ WQ___

14. I never dreamed that I could be as lonely as I am now. . . Y___ N___ WQ___

S 15. When you meet someone new do you have a hard time
       thinking of things to say?. . . . . .Y___ N___ WQ___

16. I can no longer do any kind of useful work. . . . . .Y___ N___ WQ___

17. I have enough money to get along. . . . . .Y___ N___ WQ___

P 18. Do you agree with this--? Most people try to do an
       honest day's work for a day's pay. . . . . .Y___ N___ WQ___

19. I have no use for religion. . . . . .Y___ N___ WQ___

20. My life is meaningless now. . . . . .Y___ N___ WQ___

S 21. Do you have a hard time making new friends?. . . . . . . Y___ N___ WQ___

22. I am just as happy as when I was younger. . . . . .Y___ N___ WQ___

23. I am perfectly satisfied with the way my family treats me . .Y___ N___ WQ___

P 24. Most people get ahead because they have pull. . . . . . . .Y___ N___ WQ___

25. I never felt better in my life. . . . . .Y___ N___ WQ___

26. I would be happier if I could see my friends more often. . . Y___ N___ WQ___

S 27. Would you like to belong to a lot of clubs?. . . . . Y___ N___ WQ___

28. I am satisfied with the work I now do. . . . . Y___ N___ WQ___

29. I haven't a cent in the world. . . . . Y___ N___ WQ___

P 30. Do you think you have gotten all you deserve out of life?.. Y___ N___ WQ___

31. Religion is a great comfort to me. . . . . Y___ N___ WQ___

32. The days are too short for all I want to do. . . . . Y___ N___ WQ___

S 33. Would you rather work alone than with somebody?. . . . . . . Y___ N___ WQ___

34. My life could be happier than it is now. . . . . Y___ N___ WQ___

35. I wish my family would pay more attention to me. . . . . . . Y___ N___ WQ___

P 36. Do you agree with this--? If you want a thing done
right you have to do it yourself. . . . . Y___ N___ WQ___

37. If I can't feel better soon, I would just as soon die. . . . Y___ N___ WQ___

38. I have no one to talk to about personal things. . . . . . . .Y___ N___ WQ___

S 39. Do people think you're a sociable person?. . . . . Y___ N___ WQ___

40. I have no work to look forward to.. . . . . .Y___ N___ WQ___

41. All my needs are cared for. . . . . .Y___ N___ WQ___

P 42. Do you think some people pay too much attention to
your business?. . . . . .Y___ N___ WQ___

43. Religion doesn't mean much to me. . . . . .Y___ N___ WQ___

44. Sometimes I feel there's just no point in living. . . . . .Y___ N___ WQ___

S 45. Do other people say that it is hard to get to know you?.. . .Y___ N___ WQ___

46. I seem to have less and less reason to live. . . . . Y___ N___ WQ___

47. I think my family is the finest in the world. . . . . Y___ N___ WQ___

P 48. Do you agree with this--? Most people are out to get
more than they give. . . . . .Y___ N___ WQ___

49. When I was younger, I felt a little better than I do now. . .Y___ N___ WQ___

50. I have so few friends that I am lonely much of the time. . . .Y___ N___ WQ___

S 51. When you are in a group, would you rather listen than talk? .Y___ N___ WQ___

52. I get badly flustered when I have to hurry with my work. . . Y___ N___ WQ___

53. I am provided with many home comforts. . . . . Y___ N___ WQ___

P 54. Do you agree with this--? Almost anyone, even poor
people, can get a square deal in court. . . . . Y___ N___ WQ___

55. I don't rely on prayer to help me. . . . . Y___ N___ WQ___

56. My life is still busy and useful. . . . . .Y___ N___ WQ___

S 57. Do you like to be with people? . . . . Y___ N___ WQ___

58. These are the best years of my life . . . . Y___ N___ WQ___

   59. My family is always trying to boss me. . . . . Y___ N___ WQ___

P 60. Do you think some people go out of their way to make
        things hard for you?. . . . . .Y___ N___ WQ___

   61. My health is just beginning to be a burden to me. . . . . . .Y___ N___ WQ___

   62. My many friends make my life happy and cheerful. . . . . . Y___ N___ WQ___

S 63. Do people seem to enjoy being with you?. . . . . Y___ N___ WQ___

   64. I do better work now than ever before. . . . . Y___ N___ WQ___

   65. I have everything that money can buy. . . . . Y___ N___ WQ___

P 66. Do you agree with this--? Most people tell a lie
        now and then to get ahead. . . . . Y___ N___ WQ___

   67. Religion is the most important thing in my life. . . . . . Y___ N___ WQ___

   68. This is the most useful period of my life . . . . Y___ N___ WQ___

P 69. Do you agree with this--? Nearly everybody tries to do
        the right things if he is given the chance. . . . . Y___ N___ WQ___

   70. My life is full of worry. . . . . .Y___ N___ WQ___

   71. I get more love and affection now than I ever did before. . .Y___ N___ WQ___

   72. I still feel young and full of spirit. . . . . Y___ N___ WQ___

   73. I have all the good friends anyone could wish. . . . . . . Y___ N___ WQ___

   74. I have more free time than I know how to use. . . . . Y___ N___ WQ___

   75. I have to watch how I spend every penny. . . . . Y___ N___ WQ___

   76. Religion is only one of many interests . . . . Y___ N___ WQ___

   77. I can't help feeling now that my life is not very useful. . Y___ N___ WQ___

   78. My family does not really care for me. . . . . Y___ N___ WQ___

   79. My life is so enjoyable that I almost wish it would go
        on forever. . . . . .Y___ N___ WQ___

*Items from Opinion Conformity Scale.

Thanks much for your cooperation--for your time and interest.

(Verify 1955 information on household--update to 1956.)
(Be certain to sign your name on the project slip and leave it with
 interviewee.)

Project Information

    You know people are living longer these days and it is important to know
what older people are doing and thinking. It is important, too, that we know
what people of all ages believe is good for our senior citizens. The Committee
for Study of Adulthood at The Pennsylvania State University is conducting such
a study. If you would like more information about the study, please write:

                    Dr. Joseph H. Britton
                    Committee for Study of Adulthood
                    The Pennsylvania State University
                    University Park, Pennsylvania 16802

Interviewer:

Appendix E
Thematic Apperception Test Rating Sheet
and Outline for TAT Analysis

The Pennsylvania State University

Thematic Apperception Test
Rating Sheet

Judge No._____   1956 Schedule No._____

Date_____19_____   Male   Female

Card: 7BM   6BM   10

Number of words without prodding_____
Number of words with prodding_____
Total number of words_____

I. Story as a Whole

    1. Many ideas   7 6 5 4 3 2 1   Few ideas_____

    2. Rambling   1 2 3 4 5 4 7   Succinct_____

    3. Outcome agreeable 7 6 5 4 3 2 1   Outcome disagreeable_____

    4. Directions followed7 6 5 4 3 2 1   Directions ignored_____

    5. Inappropriate   1 2 3 4 5 6 7   Appropriate_____

    6. Outcome definite   7 6 5 4 3 2 1   Outcome indefinite_____

    7. Unimaginative   1 2 3 4 5 6 7   Imaginative_____

    8. Fitting   7 6 5 4 3 2 1   Bizarre_____

    9. Disorganized   1 2 3 4 5 6 7   Organized_____

    10. Happy outcome   7 6 5 4 3 2 1   Unhappy outcome_____

    11. Unsuitable   1 2 3 4 5 6 7   Suitable_____

    12. Original   7 6 5 4 3 2 1   Stereotyped_____

    13. Unpleasant ending 1 2 3 4 5 6 7   Pleasant ending_____

    14. Rich,   7 6 5 4 3 2 1   Constricted_____

    15. Coherent   7 6 5 4 3 2 1   Incoherent_____

II. Main Older Person In Story   (Unclear: Sex of identificant M   F   )

    1. Persuasive   7 6 5 4 3 2 1   Ineffective_____

    2. Controlled   7 6 5 4 3 2 1   Impulsive_____

    3. Confident   7 6 5 4 3 2 1   Unassured_____

    4. Important   7 6 5 4 3 2 1   Unimportant_____

    5. Alert   7 6 5 5 3 2 1   Listless_____

6.	Clever	7 6 5 4 3 2 1	Foolish_____
7.	Accepted	7 6 5 4 3 2 1	Rejected_____
8.	Friendly	7 6 5 4 3 2 1	Unfriendly_____
9.	Liberal	7 6 5 4 3 2 1	Stingy_____
10.	Sad	1 2 3 4 5 6 7	Happy_____
11.	Acquiescent	1 2 3 4 5 6 7	Assertive_____
12.	Spontaneous	1 2 3 4 5 6 7	Restrained_____
13.	Anxious	1 2 3 4 5 6 7	Secure_____
14.	Low rank	1 2 3 4 5 6 7	High rank_____
15.	Slow	1 2 3 4 5 6 7	Spry_____
16.	Unintelligent	1 2 3 4 5 6 7	Intelligent_____
17.	Loved	7 6 5 4 3 2 1	Unloved_____
18.	Belligerent	1 2 3 4 5 6 7	Accepting_____
19.	Miserly	1 2 3 4 5 6 7	Generous_____
20.	Euphoric mood	7 6 5 4 3 2 1	Dysphoric mood_____
21.	Influential	7 6 5 4 3 2 1	Powerless_____
22.	Constricted emotion	7 6 5 4 3 2 1	Labile emotion_____
23.	Independent	7 6 5 4 3 2 1	Dependent_____
24.	Inconsequential	1 2 3 4 5 6 7	Consequential_____
25.	Swift	7 6 5 4 3 2 1	Sluggish_____
26.	Bright	7 6 5 4 3 2 1	Dull_____
27.	Useless	1 2 3 4 5 6 7	Useful_____
28.	Aggressive	1 2 3 4 5 6 7	Passive_____
29.	Fussy	1 2 3 4 5 6 7	Permissive_____
30.	Happy	7 6 5 4 3 2 1	Unhappy_____
31.	Initiates action	7 6 5 4 3 2 1	Recipient of action_____
32.	Adequate	7 6 5 4 3 2 1	Inadequate_____
33.	Inferior status	1 2 3 4 5 6 7	Superior status_____
34.	Passive	1 2 3 4 5 6 7	Active_____
35.	Carefree	7 6 5 4 3 2 1	Fault-finding_____
36.	Fearful	1 2 3 4 5 6 7	Absence of fear_____
37.	Satisfied	7 6 5 4 3 2 1	Complaining_____
38.	Melancholy	1 2 3 4 5 6 7	Gay_____
39.	Demanding	1 2 3 4 5 6 7	Not demanding_____

40.	Freedom from narcissism	7 6 5 4 3 2 1	Narcissistic_____
41.	Seclusive	1 2 3 4 5 6 7	Companionable_____
42.	Joyful	7 6 5 4 3 2 1	Gloomy_____
43.	Trusting	7 6 5 4 3 2 1	Doubting_____
44.	Adaptive	7 6 5 4 3 2 1	Unyielding_____
45.	Crabby	1 2 3 4 5 6 7	Pleasant_____
46.	Self-centered	1 2 3 4 5 6 7	Interested in others_____
47.	Withdrawn	1 2 3 4 5 6 7	Sociable_____
48.	Accepting	7 6 5 4 3 2 1	Suspicious_____
49.	Rigid	1 2 3 4 5 6 7	Flexible_____
50.	Gregarious	7 6 5 4 3 2 1	Retiring_____

Outline for TAT Analysis[1]

CF 46   6/57
Jackson - Britton

I. Story as a whole   Items

    A. General nature of story . . . . 1,7,(12),14
    B. Organization 2,9,15
    C. Nature of the outcome . . . . 3,(6),10,13
    D. Following of directions 4
    E. Appropriateness of story 5,8,11

II. Main older person in story

    A. Adequacy in initiating action 1,11,21,31
    B. Spontaniety and control 2,12,22
    C. Confidence and adequacy 3,13,23,32,36
    D. Hierarchical status 4,14,24,33
    E. Activity 5,15,25,34
    F. Intellectual functioning 6,16,26
    G. Interpersonal acceptance 7,17,27
    H. Aggression 8,18,28
    J. Stereotypes
        1. Penurious 9,19
        2. Fussy 29,35,37,45
        3. Self-demanding 39
        4. Self-centered 40,46
        5. Reclusive 41,47,50
        6. Suspicious 43,48
        7. Rigid 44,49
    K. Happiness 10,20,30,38,42

---

[1]Scales under I and II - J were omitted in the scoring procedure; therefore, 34 items (Dimension Scales II-A - H and II-K) were included. No use was made of the dimensions scales here.

Appendix F
The Judge's Rating

The Pennsylvania State University

1956 Schedule No._____

Rater_____

Date_____

Male   Female

The Judge's Rating
(The Cavan Adjustment Rating Scale)

The Cavan Adjustment Rating Scale consists of six rating scales followed by a master rating. The first three scales have to do with primary and secondary relations and with activities outside of groups. The next three scales represent certain attitudes that are central to personal adjustment.

The master scale is a flexible summary of the six more specific scales. On the basis of the six scales, the rater arrives at a decision about the general degree of personal adjustment, but he takes into account other things he knows about the individual and he weighs the separate scales in accordance with what seems to him their importance in the individual case.

1. Primary or personal, intimate contacts

0 . 1	2 . 3	4 . 5	6 . 7	8 . 9
Alone in world; no family, relatives, friends	Infrequent contacts; perhaps lives alone, sees family sometimes; or lives with but not closely incorporated	Frequent contacts or lives with and is functioning member of intimate groups	Almost daily contacts; helps determine group actions	Daily contacts; group probably of long standing; closely incorporated into group life; important in determining group actions

2. Secondary or more formal and specialized contacts

0 . 1	2 . 3	4 . 5	6 . 7	8 . 9
In no groups, no reading, no radio. Complete social isolation	Perhaps one group or irregular group contacts; occasional radio	Several groups, regular participation, some reading or radio, probably favorite programs	More than several groups; regular participation, chief interest is these contacts; much reading, radio, television	Time filled with many groups, much reading, many radio programs. Always on the go or occupied with reading, radio

3. Activities outside groups

0 . 1 . 2 . 3 . 4 . 5 . 6 . 7 . 8 . 9

1	3	6–7	8–9
"Nothing to do." Few activities; has too much free time	Some daily activities, probably a hobby, but time for group life also	Preponderance of time in daily activities, hobbies, etc.	Time filled with daily activities, hobbies, plans to exclusion of group activities

4. Attitude of emotional security in small group (or religion)

0 . 1 . 2 . 3 . 4 . 5 . 6 . 7 . 8 . 9

1	3	5	6–7	8–9
Feels unwanted, "nobody cares," pushed aside	Some uneasiness about being wanted	Feels comfortably secure	Feels loved above the average person	Feels greatly beloved; wanted, gets lavish attention

5. Status or feeling of importance

0 . 1 . 2 . 3 . 4 . 5 . 6 . 7 . 8 . 9

1	3	4–5	6–7	8–9
Feels looked down on, low status, feels disrespect on the part of others	Feels others are indifferent to him, disregard his opinions, etc.	Feels he is of some importance, but no more so than others	Feels he is looked up to slightly; shown some respect	Feels he is in position of high status; opinions sought and followed

6. Happiness and contentment

0 . 1 . 2 . 3 . 4 . 5 . 6 . 7 . 8 . 9

1	3	4–5	6–7	8–9
Unhappy, discontented, worried fearful, frustrated	Inclined to be unhappy, to worry, some frustrations	Generally happy, contented, unworried	Always happy, unworried, contented	Very happy, exultant, "happiest time," great contentment

7. Master rating on personal adjustment

0 . 1 . 2 . 3 . 4 . 5 . 6 . 7 . 8 . 9

1	3	4–5	6–7	8–9
Seriously maladjusted socially, many gaps in social life, much tent emotional disturbance	Meagre social life some emotional disturbance and discontent	Moderate social life; if lacks one type, compensates with other types, if emotional disturbance, readily adjusted	Fairly well-developed social life, no serious gaps, positive emotional reactions	Well-rounded social life of all types, very good emotional reactions

Appendix G
Interviewer's Report

The Pennsylvania State University

Interviewer's Report

1956 Schedule No._____
Interviewee_____
Interviewer_____
Date_____

1. <u>Respondent</u>: Available_____
   Unavailable_____Reason_____
   _____

   Recommendation: Call back_____
   Different interviewer_____
   Omit_____

2. <u>Interview</u>: Completed_____
   Not completed_____Reason_____
   _____

   Recommendation:_____

3. Total length of interview_____

4. Total time of distractions and interruptions_____

Evaluation of respondent's behavior (Encircle rating):

5. Vision. . . . . . .Poor. 1   2   3   4   5. . . . . . .Good

6. Hearing . . . . . .Poor. 1   2   3   4   5. . . . . . .Good

7. Attention and   Mind wanders
   concentration. .   frequently .. .1   2   3   4   5. . . . . . .Attended
                                                                    entire
                                                                    interview

8. Interaction with   Very
   interviewer. . . .No contact. . . .1   2   3   4   5. . . . . . responsive

9. Interest. . . . . .Very casual   Intense
                      interest . . .1   2   3   4   5. . . . . . interest

10. Cooperativeness . . Barely Civil . .1   2   3   4   5. . . . . . Went out of
                                                                    his way to
                                                                    be helpful

11. Evaluation of other persons in household (friendliness, cooperativeness, helpfulness to interviewer):

12. Information pertinent to personal adjustment of interviewee not covered above:

13. Other comments or impressions of total interview and situation:

Appendix H
Community Rating, Panelist Interveiw

The Pennsylvania State University

Community Rating   Panelist No._____
Panelist Interview   Interviewee_____
                                          Interviewer_____
                                          Date_____

We are interested in learning something of how the community thinks about
certain older persons. To help us in this process, will you tell us first
some things about yourself?

1. How long have you lived in this community?

2. How old were you on your last birthday?

3. What work have you done most of the time during your adult years? (Tell what
   kind of work it was--for example, labor on a road construction gang, teller
   in a bank, etc.)

4. Are you working now?

        Yes, full-time..........____
        Yes, part-time..........____
        No......................____

5. If you are working what do you do?

6. What was the last grade of school that you finished?

7. To what social and civic community organizations do you now belong?

8. Are you an officer in any of these organizations? (List)

9. Do you now have or have you had a person 65 or older living in your home?

10. If yes, who?

11. If yes, how long has the arrangement been in effect?

12. If yes, how did it work out?

Appendix I
Organization Leader Interview

The Pennsylvania State University

Organization Leader Interview

Interviewee_____
Organization_____
Interviewer_____
Date_____

We want to know something about your organization in relation to older people. For this survey, we have arbitrarily said older people are those 65 or older.

1. About how many older persons belong to your organization? (number)

2. About what proportion is this of total membership?

3. Do you have any programs, services, or activities planned especially for older people? (describe: name, purpose, kinds of activities, number of members, frequency of meetings, etc.)

    (If no, go to #5)
4. If yes: To what extent do the older persons participate in them? (frequency, regularity, all or few, etc.)

5. Are there other activities or programs in your organization in which older persons might be included? (describe)

6. To what extent do the older persons use them?

7. Does your local group help maintain a home for the aged?

    (If no, go to #11)
8. What sort of place is it? (describe location, size, support, etc.)

9. What kinds of people go there? (rich, poor, ones with no family, etc.)

10. About how many older persons from Pennsboro and Green Township have gone there in the last five years? (number, names?)

11. As you see it, are there any special problems which older people present in your organization? What might they be?

12. Are there any particular advantages which older persons bring to the organization? As you see it, what might they be?

196

Appendix J
Professional Services Interview

The Pennsylvania State University

Professional Services Interview

Interviewee_____
Position_____
Interviewer_____
Date_____

We want to know something about your professional activities in relation to older people. For this survey, we have arbitrarily said older people are those 65 or older.

1. About how many older persons come to you for professional help? (number)

2. About what proportion is this of the total number who come?

3. What sorts of problems do they present? (describe)

4. About what proportion of the older persons you deal with have problems which you think are primarily psychological?

5. We'd like to know what some of these problems are like. Will you tell me about some of them? (describe)

6. In what ways are these problems different from those of younger persons? (describe how)

7. In general, what do you see as possible solutions for these problems? (check problems in 3 and 5)

Appendix K
Community Rating, Q-Sort Items

Community Rating, Q-Sort Items

I-A. Almost everyone respects him.

  B. Most people respect him.

  C. Only his friends respect him.

  D. Few people respect him.

  E. Hardly anyone respects him.

II-A. His opinion is almost always asked.

  B. His opinion is thought of as important.

  C. His opinion is asked only on a certain few things.

  D. His opinion is not thought of as important.

  E. His opinion is almost never asked.

III-A. He almost always does what he's supposed to do.

  B. He usually does the right thing.

  C. He does the right thing when he thinks it's important.

  D. He sometimes does things he shouldn't.

  E. He almost never does what he's supposed to do.

IV-A. He is unusually considerate of others.

  B. Helpful to others most of the time.

  C. Will help when asked.

  D. He helps others only when it's to his advantage.

  E. Hardly ever helps anyone else.

V-A. Almost everyone he knows is his friend.

  B. He has more friends than most people.

  C. Has a good number of friends.

  D. Has few friends.

  E. Has almost no friends.

Appendix L
Community Rating, Q-Sort Recording Sheet

The Pennsylvania State University

Community Rating,
Q-Sort Recording Sheet
25 Names (1956)

Panelist No._____
Interviewer_____
Date_____

These cards have the names of 25 people you have said you know. We want to describe these persons as other people in their community see them. We are going to ask you to sort these names (hold up cards) certain ways. This information will be coded so your name, and the names of those you sort, will never be used. All your answers will be kept strictly confidential.

Underneath each of these cards (spread I - A,B,C,D,E cards left to right in front of the panelist), will you put the right number of cards--the number shown under the statement. It will probably be easier if you first sort the ones that seem to fit quickly and then put the others in the groups that fit the best.

I.
A	B	C	D	E
1._____	1._____	1._____	1._____	1._____
2._____	2._____	2._____	2._____	2._____
3._____	3._____	3._____	3._____	3._____
	4._____	4._____	4._____	
	5._____	5._____	5._____	
		6._____		
		7._____		
		8._____		
		9._____		(Shuffle cards before handing them to the panelist again)

II.
A	B	C	D	E
1._____	1._____	1._____	1._____	1._____
2._____	2._____	2._____	2._____	2._____
3._____	3._____	3._____	3._____	3._____
	4._____	4._____	4._____	
	5._____	5._____	5._____	
		6._____		
		7._____		
		8._____		
		9._____		(Shuffle cards)

III.
A	B	C	D	E
1._____	1._____	1._____	1._____	1._____
2._____	2._____	2._____	2._____	2._____
3._____	3._____	3._____	3._____	3._____
	4._____	4._____	4._____	
	5._____	5._____	5._____	
		6._____		
		7._____		
		8._____		
		9._____		(Shuffle cards)

IV.   <u>A</u>   <u>B</u>   <u>C</u>   <u>D</u>   <u>E</u>

A	B	C	D	E
1.___	1.___	1.___	1.___	1.___
2.___	2.___	2.___	2.___	2.___
3.___	3.___	3.___	3.___	3.___
	4.___	4.___	4.___	
	5.___	5.___	5.___	
		6.___		
		7.___		
		8.___		
		9.___		(Shuffle cards)

V.   <u>A</u>   <u>B</u>   <u>C</u>   <u>D</u>   <u>E</u>

A	B	C	D	E
1.___	1.___	1.___	1.___	1.___
2.___	2.___	2.___	2.___	2.___
3.___	3.___	3.___	3.___	3.___
	4.___	4.___	4.___	
	5.___	5.___	5.___	
		6.___		
		7.___		
		8.___		
		9.___		

(Be sure to thank the interviewee for his help!)

References

Allport, G. W. *Becoming: Basic considerations for a psychology of personality.* New Haven: Yale University Press, 1955.

Anderson, J. E. *A survey of children's adjustment over time: A report to the people of Nobles County.* Minneapolis: University of Minnesota Press, 1959.

Anderson, J. E. Psychological research on changes and transformations during development and aging. In J. E. Birren (Ed.) *Relations of development and aging.* Springfield, Ill.: Charles C Thomas, 1964. Pp. 11-28.

Anderson, J. E. The prediction of adjustment over time. In I. Iscoe & H. W. Stevenson (Eds.), *Personality development in children.* Austin, Texas: University of Texas Press, 1960. Pp. 28-72.

Baller, W. R., Charles, D. C., & Miller, E. L. Mid-life attainment of the mentally retarded: A longitudinal study. *Genetic Psychology Monograph,* 1967, 75, 235-339.

Baltes, P. B. Longitudinal and cross-sectional sequences in the study of age and generation effects. *Human Development,* 1968, *11,* 145-171.

Baltes, P. B., Schaie, K. W., & Nardi, A. H. Age and experimental mortality in a seven-year longitudinal study of cognitive behavior. *Developmental Psychology,* 1971, 5, 18-26.

Bandura, A. *Principles of behavior modification.* New York: Holt, Rinehart & Winston, 1969.

Bandura, A., & Walters, R. H. *Social learning and personality development.* New York: Holt, Rinehart & Winston, 1963.

Barker, R. G., & Gump, P. V. *Big school, small school: High school size and student behavior.* Stanford: Stanford University Press, 1964.

Barker, R. G., & Wright, H. F. *Midwest and its children: The psychological ecology of an American town.* Evanston, Ill.: Row, Peterson, 1954.

Beard, B. B. Sensory decline in very old age. *Gerontologia Clinica,* 1969, *11,* 149-158.

Becker, H. S. Personal change in adult life. *Sociometry,* 1964, *27,* 40-50.

Becker, W. C. Consequences of different kinds of parental

discipline. In M. L. Hoffman & L. W. Hoffman, (Eds.), *Review of child development research.* Vol. 1. New York: Russell Sage, 1964. Pp. 169-208.

Beilin, H. The prediction of adjustment over a four-year interval. *Journal of Clinical Psychology*, 1957, *13*, 270-274.

Bell, R. Q. Convergence: An accelerated longitudinal approach. *Child Development*, 1953, *24*, 145-152.

Bell, R. Q. An experimental test of the accelerated longitudinal approach. *Child Development*, 1954, *25*, 281-286.

Berardo, F. M. Survivorship and social isolation: The case of the aged widower. *The Family Coordinator*, 1970, *19*, 11-25.

Berkowitz, B. Changes in intellect with age: IV. Changes in achievement and survival in older people. *Journal of Genetic Psychology*, 1965, *107*, 3-14.

Biddle, B. J., & Thomas, E. J. (Eds.) *Role theory: Concepts and research.* New York: John Wiley, 1966.

Bijou, S. W. Ages, stages, and the naturalization of human development. *American Psychologist*, 1968, *23*, 419-427.

Bijou, S. W. Experimental studies of child behavior, normal and deviant. In L. Krasner & L. P. Ullmann (Eds.), *Research in behavior modification.* New York: Holt, Rinehart & Winston, 1965. Pp. 56-81.

Birren, J. E. Principles of research on aging. In J. E. Birren (Ed.), *Handbook of aging and the individual: Psychological and biological aspects.* Chicago: University of Chicago Press, 1959. Pp. 3-42. (a).

Birren, J. E. (Ed.) *Handbook of aging and the individual: Psychological and biological aspects.* Chicago: University of Chicago Press, 1959. (b).

Birren, J. E. *The psychology of aging.* Englewood Cliffs, New Jersey: Prentice-Hall, 1964.

Birren, J. E., Butler, R. N., Greenhouse, S. W., Sokoloff, L., & Yarrow, M. R. (Eds.) *Human aging: A biological and behavioral study.* Bethesda, Maryland: U. S. Department of Health, Education, and Welfare, National Institute of Mental Health, 1962.

Bloom, B. S. *Stability and change in human characteristics.* New York: John Wiley, 1964.

Bloom, M., Blenkner, M., & Markus, E. Exploring predictors of the differential impact of relocation on the infirm aged. Paper presented at the meeting of the American Psychological Association, Washington, D.C., September 1969.

Botwinick, J. *Cognitive processes in maturity and old age.* New York: Springer, 1967.

Bortner, R. W. Adult development or idiosyncratic change? A plea for the developmental approach. *The Gerontologist,* 1966, *6,* 159-164.

Bortner, R. W. Personality and social psychology in the study of aging. *The Gerontologist,* 1967, *7,* 23-36.

Bowlby, J., Ainsworth, M., Boston, M., & Rosenbluth, D. The effects of mother-child separation: A follow-up study. *British Journal of Medical Psychology,* 1956, *29,* 211-247.

Britton, J. H. Assessment of services for the aged in rural communities. *Journal of Gerontology,* Supplement No. 2, 1958, *13,* 67-69.

Britton, J. H. Dimensions of adjustment of older adults. *Journal of Gerontology,* 1963, *18,* 60-65.

Britton, J. H. Evaluations of older adults by community members. Paper presented at the meeting of the American Psychological Association, Cincinnati, Ohio, September 1959.

Britton, J. H., & Britton, J. O. Expectations for older persons in a rural community: Solving personal problems. *Geriatrics,* 1962, *17,* 602-608.

Britton, J. H., & Britton, J. O. The middle-aged and older rural person and his family. In E. G. Youmans (Ed.), *Older rural Americans: A sociological perspective.* Lexington, Ky.: University of Kentucky Press, 1967. Pp. 44-74.

Britton, J. H., Mather, W. G., & Lansing, A. K. Expectations for older persons in a rural community: Community participation. *Rural Sociology,* 1962, *27,* 387-395.

Britton, J. H., Mather, W. G., & Lansing, A. K. Expectations for older persons in a rural community: Living arrangements and family relationships. *Journal of Gerontology,* 1961, *16,* 156-162. (a)

Britton, J. H., Mather, W. G., & Lansing, A. K. Expectations for older persons in a rural community: Work and retirement. *Geriatrics,* 1961, *16,* 664-671. (b)

Bromley, D. B., *The psychology of human ageing.* Baltimore, Md.: Penguin Books, 1966.

Brotman, H. B. Life expectancy, national and by state, 1959-61.

Useful Facts #19. Washington, D.C.: Administration on Aging, Department of Health, Education, and Welfare, April 14, 1967.

Burgess, E. W. (Ed). *Aging in Western societies.* Chicago: University of Chicago Press, 1960.

Burghardt, G. M., & Hess, E. H. Food imprinting in the snapping turtle, *Chelydra Serpentin Science*, 1966, *151*, 108-109.

Butler, R. N. Aspects of survival and adaptation in human aging. *American Journal of Psychiatry*, 1967, *123*, 1233-1243.

Bulter, R. N. The life review: An interpretation of reminiscence in the aged. *Psychiatry*, 1963, *26*, 65-76.

Cantoni, L. A study in emotional adjustment: The correlation of student and adult forms of the Bell Adjustment Inventory over a period of thirteen years. *Educational Psychology Measurement*, 1955, *15*, 137-143.

Cavan, R. S., Burgess, E. W., Havighurst, R. J., & Goldhamer, H. *Personal adjustment in old age.* Chicago: Science Research Associates, 1949.

Chown, S. M. Personality and aging. In K. W. Schaie (Ed.), *Theory and methods of research on aging: Current topics in the psychology of aging: Perception, learning, cognition, and personality.* Morgantown: West Virginia University Press, 1968. Pp. 134-157.

Clausen, J. A. Family structure, socialization, and personality. In L. W. Hoffman & M. L. Hoffman (Eds.), *Review of child development research.* Vol. 2. New York: Russell Sage, 1966. Pp. 1-53.

Copp, J. H. Three decades of change in a stable rural community. Progress Report 261, July 1965, Agricultural Experiment Station, College of Agriculture, The Pennsylvania State University, University Park, Pennsylvania.

Cowdry, E. V. (Ed.) *Problems of ageing.* Baltimore, Md.: Williams & Wilkins, 1939.

Creason, J. Joe Creason's Kentucky. Louisville (Kentucky) *Courier Journal*, September 19, 1969.

Crider, D. M. The effect of selected community attributes and individual characteristics on tracking respondents in longitudinal sociological studies. Unpublished doctoral dissertation, The Pennsylvania State University, 1969.

Cumming, E., & Henry, W. E. *Growing old.* New York: Basic Books, 1961.

Darwin, C. The origin of species. In C. W. Eliot (Ed.), *The Harvard Classics*. Vol. 11. New York: P. F. Collier & Son, 1909.

Davidson, J. D. Change in adjustment of older adults as related to situational and personal factors. Unpublished master's thesis, The Pennsylvania State University, 1963.

Davis, B. W. The prediction of life satisfaction, work satisfaction, and social mobility in early adulthood. Unpublished master's thesis, The Pennsylvania State University, 1971.

Elkind, D. Cognitive development in adolescence. In J. F. Adams (Ed.), *Understanding adolescence*. Boston: Allyn and Bacon, 1968. Pp. 128-158.

Emmerich, W. Models of continuity and change in development. Paper presented at the meeting of the Society for Research in Child Development, Santa Monica, California, March 1969.

English, H. B., & English, A. C. *A comprehensive dictionary of psychological and psychoanalytical terms: A guide to usage.* New York: Longmans, Green, 1958.

Erikson, E. H. *Childhood and society.* New York: W. W. Norton, 1950.

Garn, S. M. Body size and its implications. In L. W. Hoffman & M. L. Hoffman (Eds.), *Review of child development research.* Vol. 2. New York: Russell Sage, 1966. Pp. 529-561.

Goldfarb, N. *An introduction to longitudinal statistical analysis: The method of repeated observations from a fixed sample.* Glencoe, Ill.: Free Press, 1960.

Guilford, J. P., & Zimmerman, W. S. *The Guilford-Zimmerman Temperament Survey.* Beverly Hills, California: Sheridan Supply Co., 1949.

Hall, C. S., & Lindzey, G. *Theories of personality.* (2nd ed.) New York: John Wiley, 1970.

Harlan, W. H. Social status of the aged in three Indian villages. *Vita Humana*, 1964, 7, 239-252.

Harlow, H. F., Dodsworth, R. O., & Harlow, M. K. Total social isolation in monkeys. *Proceedings of the National Academy of Science*, 1965, 54, 90-97.

Harris, C. W. (Ed.). *Problems in measuring change.* Madison: University of Wisconsin Press, 1963.

Hartman, H., Kris, E., & Lowenstein, R. Comments on the formation of psychic structure. *Psychoanalytic study of the child*. Vol. II. New York: International Universities Press, 1946. Pp. 11-38.

Harvard team blasts traditional school. *Report on Education Research, July 21, 1971, 3 (15), 10-11* (Capitol Publications, 2430 Pennsylvania Avenue, N.W., Washington, D.C.).

Havighurst, R. J. Validity of the Chicago Attitude Inventory as a measure of personal adjustment in old age. *Journal of Abnormal and Social Psychology*, 1951, *46*, 24-29.

Havighurst, R. J. *Human development and education*. New York: Longmans, Green, 1953.

Havighurst, R. J., & Albrecht, R. *Older people*. New York: Longmans, Green, 1953.

Havighurst, R. J., Bowman, P. H., Liddle, G. P., Matthews, C. V., & Pierce, J. V. *Growing up in River City*. New York: John Wiley, 1962.

Heath, D. H. *Explorations of maturity: Studies of mature and immature college men*. New York: Appleton-Century-Crofts, 1965.

Hertz, M. R., & Baker, E. Personality changes in adolescence. *Rorschach Research Exchange*, 1941, *5*, 30.

Increase in death rates among the population of a home for the aged following relocation. *Geriatric Focus*, 1969, *8*, 2 (Knoll Pharmaceutical Company, Orange, New Jersey).

Inkeles, A., & Levinson, D. J. National character: The study of modal personality and sociocultural systems. In G. Lindzey & E. Aronson (Eds.), *The handbook of social psychology* (2nd ed.). Vol. IV. Reading, Mass.: Addison-Wesley, 1969. Pp. 418-506.

Jarvik, L. F. Survival and psychological aspects of ageing in man. *Symposium of Social and Experimental Biology*, 1967, *21*, 463-482.

Jarvik, L. F., & Falek, A. Intellectual stability and survival in the aged. *Journal of Gerontology*, 1963, *18*, 173-176.

Jarvik, L. F., Kallman, F. J., & Falek, A. Intellectual changes in aging twins. *Journal of Gerontology*, 1962, *17*, 289-294.

Jayaswal, S. R., & Stott, L. H. Persistence and change in personality from childhood to adulthood. *Merrill Palmer Quarterly*, 1955, *1*, 47-56.

Jones, H. E. Consistency and change in early maturity. *Vita Humana*, 1958, *1*, 43-51.

Jones, H. E. The longitudinal method in the study of personality. In I. Iscoe & H. W. Stevenson (Eds.). *Personality development in children.* Austin, Texas: University of Texas Press, 1960. Pp. 3-27.

Kagan, J. Continuity in development. Paper presented at the meeting of the Society for Research in Child Development, Santa Monica, California, March 1969.

Kelly, E. L. Consistency of the adult personality. *American Psychologist,* 1955, *10,* 659-681.

Kessen, W. Research design in the study of developmental problems. In P. H. Mussen (Ed.). *Handbook of research methods in child development.* New York: John Wiley, 1960. Pp. 36-70.

Kitagawa, E. M., & Hauser, P. M. Education differentials in mortality by cause of death, United States, 1960. *Demography,* 1968, *5,* 318-353.

Kleemeier, R. W. Intellectual changes in the senium or death and the I.Q. Paper presented at the meeting of the American Psychological Association, New York, September 1961.

Kleemeier, R. W. Intellectual change in the senium. *Proceedings of the Statistics Section of the American Statistical Association,* 1962. Pp. 290-295.

Kleemeier, R. W., Justiss, W. A., Rich, T. A., & Jones, A. W. Intellectual changes in an aged group. 12th Annual Report. Orange Park, Florida: Moosehaven Research Laboratory, 1961.

Kluckhohn, C., & Murray, H. A. Personality formation: The determinants. In C. Kluckhohn & H. A. Murray (Eds.), *Personality in nature, society, and culture.* New York: Alfred A. Knopf, 1949. Pp. 35-48.

Kodlin, D., & Thompson, D. J. An appraisal of the longitudinal approach to studies in growth and development. *Monograph of the Society for Research in Child Development,* 1958, *32* (No. 67).

Kraus, A. A., & Lilienfeld, A. M. Some epidemiologic aspects of the high mortality rate in the young widowed group. *Journal of Chronic Diseases,* 1959, *10,* 207-217.

Kuhlen, R. G. Developmental changes in motivation during the adults years. In J. E. Birren (Ed.), *Relations of development*

and aging. Springfield, Illinois: Charles C Thomas, 1964. Pp.
209-246. (a)

Kuhlen, R. G., Personality change with age. In P. Worchel & D.
Byrne (Eds.), *Personality change.* New York: John Wiley,
1964. Pp. 524-555. (b)

Kuo, Z-Y. *The dynamics of behavior development: An epigenetic
view.* New York: Random House, 1967.

Lansing, A. K. Behavior of older persons as viewed by people in a
rural Pennsylvania community. Unpublished master's thesis,
The Pennsylvania State University, 1956.

Lawton, M. P. Ecology and aging. In L. A. Pastalan & D. H. Carson
(Eds.), *Spatial behavior of older people.* Ann Arbor, Michigan:
Institute of Gerontology, University of Michigan-Wayne State
University, 1970. Pp. 40-67.

Lidz, T. *The person: His development throughout the life cycle.*
New York: Basic Books, 1968.

Lieberman, M. A. Observations on death and dying. *The Gerontologist,* 1966, *6,* 70-73.

Lieberman, M. A. Psychological correlates of impending death:
Some preliminary observations. *Journal of Gerontology,* 1965,
20, 182-190.

Lieberman, M. A. The relationship of mortality rates to entering a
home for the aged. *Geriatrics,* 1961, *16,* 515-519.

Lieberman, M. A., & Coplan, A. S. Distance from death as a
variable in the study of aging. *Developmental Psychology,*
1969, *2,* 71-84.

Lieberman, M. A., & Lakin, M. On becoming an institutionalized
aged person. In W. Donahue, C. Tibbits, & R. Williams (Eds.),
Processes of aging: Social and psychological perspectives. Vol.
I. New York: Atherton, 1963. Pp. 475-503.

Lindzey, G., & Byrne, D. Measurement of social choice and
interpersonal attractiveness. In G. Lindzey & E. Aronson
(Eds.), *Handbook of social psychology.* Vol. II. *Research
methods.* (2nd ed.) Reading, Mass.: Addison-Wesley, 1968. Pp.
452-525.

Maas, H. The young adult adjustment of war-time residential
nursery children. *Child Welfare,* 1963, *42,* 57-72.

Maccoby, E. E. Tracing individuality within age-related change.
Paper presented at the meeting of the Society for Research in
Child Development, Santa Monica, California, March 1969.

Maddi, S. R. *Personality theories: A comparative analysis.* Homewood, Illinois: Dorsey Press, 1968.

McClearn, G. E. Genetics and behavior development. In M. L. Hoffman & L. W. Hoffman (Eds.), *Review of child development research.* Vol. 1. New York: Russell Sage, 1964. Pp. 433-480.

McMahan, C. A., & Ford, T. R. Surviving the first five years of retirement. *Journal of Gerontology,* 1955, *10,* 212-216.

Metropolitan Life Insurance Company. Cardiac mortality and socioeconomic status. *Statistical Bulletin,* 1967, *48* (June), 9.

Metropolitan Life Insurance Company. Cirrhosis of the liver and socioeconomic status. *Statistical Bulletin,* 1968, *49* (June), 4. (a)

Metropolitan Life Insurance Company. Diabetes and socioeconomic level. *Statistical Bulletin,* 1968, *49* (August), 5. (b)

Metropolitan Life Insurance Company. Longevity dips in 1968. *Statistical Bulletin,* 1969, *50* (June), 7-9.

Metropolitan Life Insurance Company. Mortality from cerebral vascular diseases. *Statistical Bulletin,* 1968, *49* (September), 7. (c)

Milne, L. J., & Milne, M. *Patterns of survival.* Englewood Cliffs, N. J.: Prentice-Hall, 1967.

Mischel, W. Continuity and change in personality. *American Psychologist,* 1969, *24,* 1012-1018.

Murray, H. A. *Thematic Apperception Test.* Cambridge Mass.: Harvard University Press, 1943.

Mussen, P. H. *Psychological development of the child.* Englewood Cliffs, N. J.: Prentice-Hall, 1963.

Nagel, E. Determinism and development. In D. B. Harris (Ed.), *The concept of development: An issue in the study of human behavior.* Minneapolis: University of Minnesota Press, 1957.

Neugarten, B. L. Adult personality: A developmental view. *Human Development,* 1966, *9,* 61-73.

Neugarten, B. L. Adult personality: Toward a psychology of the life cycle. In B. L. Neugarten (Ed.), *Middle age and aging: A reader in social psychology.* Chicago: University of Chicago Press, 1968. Pp. 137-147.

Neugarten, B. L. Continuities and discontinuities of psychological issues into adult life. *Human Development,* 1969, *12,* 121-130.

Neugarten, B. L., & Associates. *Personality in middle and late life: Empirical studies.* New York: Atherton Press, 1964.

Neugarten, B. L., Havighurst, R. J., & Tobin, S. S. The measurement of life satisfaction. *Journal of Gerontology*, 1961, *16*, 134-143.

Oppenheimer, J. J., & Wood, P. B. *A summary of the final report of the summer scholarship program for high school juniors— 1957-1961*. Louisville, Ky.: College of Arts and Sciences, University of Louisville, 1967. (a)

Oppenheimer, J. J., & Wood, P. B. *A supplementary report to the final report, summer scholarship program for high school juniors—1957-1961*. Louisville, Ky.: College of Arts and Sciences, University of Louisville, 1967. (b)

Oppenheimer, J. J., & Wood, P. B. *Follow-up report of the summer scholarship program for high school juniors—1957-1961*. Louisville, Ky.: College of Arts and Sciences, University of Louisville, 1966.

Osborn, F. *The future of human heredity: An introduction to eugenics in modern society.* New York: Weybright & Talley, 1968.

Palmore, E. Physical, mental and social factors in predicting longevity. In E. Palmore (Ed.), *Normal aging: Reports from the Duke Longitudinal Study, 1955-1969.* Durham, N. C.: Duke University Press, 1970.

Peck R. Psychological developments in the second half of life. In J. E. Anderson (Ed.), *Psychological aspects of aging.* Washington: American Psychological Association, 1956. Pp. 42-53.

Perlman, H. H. *Persona: Social role and personality.* Chicago: University of Chicago Press, 1968.

Pollak, O. *Social adjustment in old age: A research planning report.* New York: Social Science Research Council, 1948.

Reimanis, G., & Green, R. F. Imminence of death and intellectual decrement in the aging. *Devlopmental Psychology*, 1971, *5*, 270-272.

Riegel, K. F., & Riegel, R. M. Development, dropout and death. Paper presented at the meeting of the Gerontological Society, Toronto, October 1970.

Riegel, K. F., Riegel, R. M., & Meyer, G. Sociopsychological factors of aging: A cohort-sequential analysis. *Human Development*, 1967, *10*, 27-56. (a)

Riegel, K. F., Riegel, R. M., & Meyer, G. A study of the dropout rates in longitudinal reserach on aging and the prediction of death. *Journal of Personality and Social Psychology*, 1967, *5*, 342-348. (b)

Robins, L. N. *Deviant children grown up: A sociological and psychiatric study of sociopathic personality.* Baltimore, Md.: Williams & Wilkins, 1966.

Sanderson, R. E., & Inglis, J. Learning and mortality in elderly psychiatric patients. *Journal of Gerontology*, 1961, *16*, 375-376.

Sanford, N. *Self and society: Social change and individual development.* New York: Atherton Press, 1966.

Sarbin, T. R., & Allen, V. L. Role theory. In G. Lindzey & E. Aronson (Eds.), *The handbook of social psychology.* (2nd ed.) Vol. I. Reading, Mass.: Addison-Wesley, 1968. Pp. 488-567.

Schaie, K. W. Age changes and age differences. *The Gerontologist*, 1967, *7*, 128-132.

Schaie, K. W. A general model for the study of developmental problems. *Psychological Bulletin*, 1965, *64*, 92-107.

Schaie, K. W. Cultural change and repeated assessment in the study of the adult personality. Paper presented at the meeting of the American Psychological Association, Washington, D.C., September 1971.

Schaie, K. W. Generational vs. ontogenetic components of change: A second follow-up. Paper presented at the meeting of the American Psychological Association, Washington, D.C., September 1971.

Scheibel, M. E., & Scheibel, A. B. Some neural substrates of postnatal development. In M. L. Hoffman & L. W. Hoffman (Eds.), *Review of child development research.* Vol. 1. New York: Russell Sage, 1964. Pp. 481-519.

Shaw, B. *Man and superman: A comedy and a philosophy.* London: Archibald Constable, 1907.

Shock, N. W. *A classified bibliography of gerontology and geriatrics.* Stanford, California: Stanford University Press, 1951.

Shock, N. W. *A classified bibliography of gerontology and geriatrics. Supplement One 1949-1955.* Stanford, California: Stanford University Press, 1957.

Shock, N. W. *A classified bibliography of gerontology and geriatrics. Supplement Two 1956-1961.* Stanford, California: Stanford University Press, 1963.

Siegel, S. *Nonparametric statistics for the behavioral sciences.* New York: McGraw-Hill, 1956.

Stevenson, W. *The study of behavior: Q-technique and its methodology.* Chicago: University of Chicago Press, 1953.

Strehler, B. L. *Time, cells, and aging.* New York: Academic Press, 1962.

Streib, G. F., & Thompson, W. E. The older person in a family context. In C. Tibbitts (Ed.), *Handbook of social gerontology: Societal aspects of aging.* Chicago: University of Chicago Press, 1960. Pp. 447-488.

Strong, E. K., Jr. Permanence of interest scores over 22 years. *Journal of Applied Psychology,* 1951, *35,* 89-91.

Symonds, P. M. *Adolescent Fantasy: An investigation of the picture-story method of personality study.* New York: Columbia University Press, 1949.

Symonds, P. M., with Jensen, A. R. *From adolescent to adult.* New York: Columbia University Press, 1961.

Taylor, C. Developmental conceptions and the retirement process. In F. Carp (Ed.), *Retirement.* New York: Behavioral Publications, 1971.

Thompson, W. E. Pre-retirement anticipation and adjustment in retirement. *Journal of Social Issues,* 1958, *14,* 35-45.

Tibbitts, C. (Ed.) *Handbook of social gerontology: Societal aspects of aging.* Chicago: University of Chicago Press, 1960.

U.S. Bureau of the Census. *Statistical abstracts of the United States: 1969.* (90th ed.) Washington, D.C.: U.S. Government Printing Office, 1969.

U.S. Bureau of the Census. *U.S. census of population: 1950. Vol. II, Characteristics of the population, Part 34, Pennsylvania.* Washington, D.C.: U.S. Government Printing Office, 1952.

U.S. Bureau of the Census. *U.S. census of population: 1960. Number of inhabitants, Pennsylvania.* Final Report PC (1)-40A. Washington, D.C.: U.S. Government Printing Office, 1961.

U.S. Department of Health, Education, and Welfare, Public Health Service, National Center for Health Statistics. *Mortality trends in the United States, 1954-1963.* Series 20, No. 2, June 1966.

U.S. Senate Special Committee on Aging. *New population facts on older Americans, 1960.* Washington, D.C.: U.S. Government Printing Office, May 24, 1961.

Wechsler, D. *Manual for the Wechsler Adult Intelligence Scale.* New York: Psychological Corp., 1955.

White, R. W. *Lives in progress: A study of the natural growth of personality.* (2nd ed.) New York: Holt, Rinehart & Winston, 1966.

Williams, R. H. Changing status, roles, and relationships. In C. Tibbitts (Ed.), *Handbook of social gerontology: Societal aspects of aging.* Chicago: University of Chicago Press, 1960. Pp. 261-297.

Williams, R. H., & Wirth, C. G. *Lives through the years: Styles of life and successful aging.* New York: Atherton Press, 1965.

Willits, F. K., Crider, D. M., & Bealer, R. C. A design and assessment of techniques for locating respondents in longitudinal sociological studies. Technical Report, July 1, 1969, The Pennsylvania State University, Contract PH-43-68-76, Center for Epidemiologic Studies, National Institute of Mental Health.

Witkin, H. A., Goodenough, D. R., & Karp, S. A. Stability of cognitive style from childhood to young adulthood. *Journal of Personality and Social Psychology,* 1967, 7, 291-300.

Woodruff, D. S. Age and personality: A longitudinal study. Unpublished master's thesis, University of Southern California, 1970.

Yarrow, L. J. Personality consistency and change: An overview of some conceptual and methodological issues. *Vita Humana,* 1964, 7, 67-72.

Yarrow, M. R., Campbell, J. D., & Burton, R. V. *Child rearing: An inquiry into research and methods.* San Francisco: Jossey-Bass, 1968.

Index

A

Accomplishments, evaluation of, 66-67
Activity Inventory (Chicago), 28-29, 40, 41-42, 67-68, 151
aging and survival, 107, 109
Community Rating and, 139
inter-year correlations, 73, 74
Longitudinal Trend Scores, 75
Reputation Rating and, 130
three measurements, 67-68
Adjustment patterns, 10
See also Personality and adjustment
Adulthood, changes during, 5-6
Aging and survival, 10-12, 97-114
analysis, 101
definition, 6, 8
findings, 101-112, 153-154
attrition over the years, 101-104
interview data, 107-110
longitudinal studies, 56-57
Longitudinal Trend Scores, 111-113
maintenance and prevention of decline, 8
method and procedures, 100-101
related research, 98-100
reputations and, 132
sample bias, 104-105
in small community setting, 12-13
survey data, 105-107
survivors and nonsurvivors, 104-105
Albrecht, R., 48-49
Allen, V.L., 5
Allport, G.W., 166-167
American Psychological Association, 8
Analytic methods, 52-54
data processing, 52-53
inter-year correlations, 73-74
Longitudinal Trend Scores, 53-54
Anderson, J.E., 32, 160
Attention and concentration, 49
Attitude Inventory (Chicago), 28-29, 40, 42-43, 151

aging and survival, 107, 109
Community Rating and, 139
inter-year correlations, 73, 74
Longitudinal Trend Scores, 76
Reputation Rating and, 130
three measurements, 67-68

B

Baker, E., 160
Baller, W.R., 159
Baltes, P.B., 33, 99
Bandura, A., 5, 166
Barker, R.G., 144
Bealer, R.C., 17
Beard, B.B., 99
Becker, H.S., 5,6
Becker, W.C., 164
Behavior of older persons:
community attitudes toward, 115-127
environment and, 10
Beilin, H., 160
Bell, R.Q., 32
Berkowitz, B., 99
Biddle, B.J., 5
Bijou, S.W., 166
Birren, J.E., 2, 5, 11, 16, 32
Blenkner, M., 99
Bloom, B.S., 2, 156, 157-158, 159, 163, 164, 167
Bloom, M., 99
Bortner, R.W., 2
Botwinick, J., 112
Bowlby, J., 160
Bowman, P.H., 161
Britton, J.H., 28, 35, 45, 51, 107, 117, 141
Britton, J.O., 28, 45, 107, 141
Bromley, D.B., 6
Brotman, H.B., 57
Burgess, E.W., 41, 42, 116, 151
Burghardt, G.M., 169
Burton, R.V., 163
Butler, R.N., 5, 99